Getting Started on

HOME
LEARNING

ALSO BY REBECCA RUPP

The Complete Home Learning Sourcebook

How We Remember and Why We Forget

The Dragon of Lonely Island

Everything You Never Learned About Birds

Good Stuff

Red Oaks and Black Birches: The Science and Lore of Trees

Getting Started on

HOME LEARNING

How and Why
to Teach Your Kids
at Home

REBECCA RUPP

Three Rivers Press, NEW YORK

For Randy
For Josh, Ethan, and Caleb

Copyright © 1999 by Rebecca Rupp

Published by Three Rivers Press, 201 East 50th Street, New York, New York
10022. Member of the Crown Publishing Group.

Random House, Inc. New York, Toronto, London, Sydney, Auckland
www.randomhouse.com

THREE RIVERS PRESS is a registered trademark of Random House, Inc.

Printed in the United States of America
Design by Meryl Sussman Levavi/digitext, inc.

Library of Congress Cataloging-in-Publication Data
Rupp, Rebecca.
    Getting started on home learning : how and why to teach your kids
at home / Rebecca Rupp.—1st ed.
    1. Home schooling—United States—Handbooks, manuals, etc.
I. Title.
LC40.R85   1999
371.04'2—dc21
                                                                99-12789
                                                                   CIP

ISBN 0-609-80343-3

10 9 8 7 6 5 4 3 2 1
First Edition

ACKNOWLEDGMENTS

Many thanks to all who have helped in the preparation of this book, especially to my editors at Crown, Ayesha Pande and Alexia Brue, for their patience, advice, and senses of humor; to my agent, Joe Spieler, for his support, wisdom, and Vermont-style common sense; and to all the many homeschooling friends and associates who have shared their opinions and experiences, joys and sorrows, and triumphs and tribulations.

A special thanks, as always, goes to my family: my husband Randy, who encouraged all those explosive chemistry experiments, and our sons, Joshua, Ethan, and Caleb, who are a joy and a delight to homeschool.

CONTENTS

You are the bows from which your children as living arrows are sent forth.

KAHLIL GIBRAN

WHY HOMESCHOOL?

School-days, I believe, are the unhappiest in the whole span of human existence. They are full of dull, unintelligible tasks, new and unpleasant ordinances, brutal violations of common sense and common decency. It doesn't take a reasonably bright boy long to discover that most of what is rammed into him is nonsense and that no one really cares very much whether he learns it or not.

H. L. MENCKEN
A MENCKEN CHRESTOMATHY

Schools seem to me among the most anti-democratic, most authoritarian, most destructive, and most dangerous institutions of modern society. No other institution does more harm or more lasting harm to more people or destroys so much of their curiosity, trust, dignity, and sense of identity and worth.

JOHN HOLT
ESCAPE FROM CHILDHOOD

My grandmother wanted me to get an education, so she kept me out of school.

MARGARET MEAD
BLACKBERRY WINTER

The word *school* is fraught with associations. It conjures up idealistic Norman Rockwell images of little red schoolhouses, lunch baskets, slate pencils, and scrubbed students who really did bring apples for their teachers; it triggers a wealth of not quite so idealistic real-life memories, involving—at least on my part—the smell of gym suits, Lysol, and chalk dust, windows that could only be opened and closed by means of eight-foot wooden poles, cacophonous yellow school buses, playground bullies (Susan McConnell in first grade, an angelic platinum blond child with the strength of a gorilla), public-address-system announcements, report cards, and the blue-haired virago who taught me (and my brother) algebra. For better or for worse, the vast majority of Americans have shared this common experience: they have spent the bulk of their childhoods in schools.

Most of us entered the public school system in kindergarten at the age of five or six and proceeded, in sequential lockstep, through elementary school, middle school, and high school, learning along the way the ins and outs of reading, writing, and arithmetic, cafeteria lunches, kickball, parent-teacher conferences, peer pressure, and proms. Few of us, at the time, envisioned any other mode of learning. Kindergarten was the alphabet song; second grade, phonics; fourth, long division. By seventh grade, the day was divided up into forty-minute periods, separated by bells of the sort that alert firepersons to conflagrative disasters. The teachers stayed put; we trudged from room to room, hauling our books, notebooks, calculators, pencils, and ballpoint pens.

Classes we liked didn't last very long, but then neither did classes that we didn't, which—at least in the case of the aforementioned algebra—was a blessing, since the algebra teacher operated by sending us to the blackboard, where she relentlessly taunted those who fell apart in the midst of polynomial equations. Ninth grade was earth science; tenth, biology; eleventh, chemistry; and twelfth, if you were still determined to make a career of science, physics, which was ineptly taught by the biology teacher. If you did what you were told, you were rewarded; if you didn't, you went to the principal's office and spent your after-school hours in detention hall. If you got straight A's and excellent standardized test scores, you went to a good college and became a doctor, a lawyer, or a CEO; if you got D's and refused to take the SAT, chances were you ended up bagging groceries at the A & P. All this was a given. Life for most of us, between the ages of six and eighteen, was school.

School, in the twentieth century, has played an increasingly influential role in the shaping of American life. Not only can a child's success—or failure—in school determine the course of his or her future, but families with children of school age find the very pattern of their daily lives directed by the demands of the school system. The schools determine when kids get out of bed in the morning and when they return home in the evening, dictate what, when, and how they learn, assess their psychological and physical health, structure their social lives, and channel their moral values. And, should you object to any of the above, there's little you can do. School, in the United States, is not simply publicly available: it is mandatory. American citizens are, for the most part, strictly limited by the state in their choice of methods for educating their children. Unlike sneakers, crayons, and ice-cream-cone flavors, public education is a one-choice deal. As Henry Ford was said to have boasted of his brand-new Model T: "You can get it in any color you want—as long as it's black."

Our acceptance of *public school system* as a synonym for *education*, however, is a fairly recent phenomenon. Despite its sudden leap into the educational spotlight—with recent features in *The New York Times*, *Newsweek*, and *The Wall Street Journal*—homeschooling, as a viable means of educating the young, is far from new. Until the twentieth century, most Americans received all or part of their education at home.

Furthermore—peculiar as it may seem to generations raised in the long shadow of the public schools—the method seems to have worked. Our home-educated ancestors, historians point out, read Sir Walter Scott—hardly a lightweight author—for fun; and listened, enthralled, to hour upon hour of politically complex dialogue in the Lincoln-Douglas debates. Proponents of homeschooling often cite such notable home-taught (or at least partially home-taught) success stories as Thomas Jefferson, Abraham Lincoln, Thomas Edison, Margaret Mead, Louisa May Alcott, Andrew Wyeth, C. S. Lewis, and Albert Einstein.

There are now approximately fifty million kids of school age in the United States. Of these, about forty-five million attend public schools, five million are enrolled in private schools, and somewhere between 700,000 and 1.5 million—estimates vary—are homeschooled or taught at home, usually by their parents. Homeschooling is a rapidly growing subset of the modern educational community. Over the past two decades, more and more parents have chosen to remove their children from the school system altogether, preferring, for a variety of reasons, to take educational matters into their own hands. What began as a tiny band of nonconformists in the early 1970s is now a sizable chunk of the population. The first members of the modern homeschool movement—many of them parents who came of age in the freethinking sixties—were an eclectic band of hippies, homesteaders, and political libertarians who found that homeschooling best suited their independent and/or distinctly nonmainstream lifestyles. The second wave appeared in the 1980s, when new legislation led to the revocation of tax-exempt status for Christian schools. Many of these institutions, deprived of financial protections, promptly folded, and conservative Christians—determined to provide their children with a religious education—plunged into homeschooling. In the 1990s, as middle-class parents became increasingly dissatisfied with the academic performance and social atmosphere of the public schools, alternative educational choice, notably homeschooling—became increasingly popular. Official numbers continue to mushroom: the number of New York homeschoolers nearly tripled between 1990 and 1994; the number of Vermont homeschoolers grows by about 30 percent annually; and the homeschool population nationwide increases by 15 percent to 40 percent each year.

Sheer weight of numbers, however, does not mean that the practice of homeschooling is universally approved. The National Education Association (NEA)—the 2.4-million-member teacher's union—states unequivocally that "home education programs cannot provide the student with a comprehensive education experience." "I wouldn't want my child educated like that," stated NEA spokesperson Kathleen Lyons in a recent *New York Times* article on homeschooling. "Or to grow up in a society where the majority were educated like that. Our society is loose enough as it is. The thing that binds us together in this country is public education." The National Association of Elementary School Principals (NAESP) is also adamantly negative, strenuously advocating the prohibition of homeschooling—all forms of homeschooling—as an acceptable educational alternative. Anne Bryant of the National School Boards Association doubts that homeschooled children—deprived of the science and technology courses available in the public schools—can be academically competitive with their conventionally educated peers.

So why, despite such bad press from educational professionals, do so many families choose to homeschool? Some homeschool for religious—often fundamentalist Christian—reasons. Many of these families, a notably vocal subset of the homeschool population, object to the content of the public school curriculum: for example, the teaching of evolution, the use of texts that contain materials considered antibiblical, or the promulgation of "humanist" ethical values. About half of homeschoolers, studies suggest, cite religion as a major reason for their educational choice. Homeschoolers, however, are far from a homogeneous enclave of Christian conservatives. Despite determined organizational efforts by various political hopefuls, homeschoolers remain a philosophically and politically diverse group. Some, supporters of the educational philosophy of Ivan Illich, author of *Deschooling Society* (1970), see homeschooling as an expression of political and social freedom. Others—citing ominous statistics on school violence, teen pregnancy, and drug and alcohol abuse—want to protect their children from the negative aspects of public school socialization. Still others believe in the superiority of one-on-one tutoring over classroom instruction; or hope to encourage family solidarity; or feel that the school atmosphere stifles creativity and independent thinking. And then there's the connecting thread: most homeschoolers firmly believe that parents are ultimately responsible for the education of their children and thus should have the right to make the decisions about how, when, and where this education is provided.

Deschooling Society.
Illich, Ivan; Harper & Row, 1971.
   "We have all learned most of what we know outside school," writes Illich. "Pupils do most of their learning without, and often despite, their teachers." To learn freely and effectively, to pursue our own chosen goals, Illich argues, we must choose new learning methods and establish new forms of social institutions.

   "For us," writes a homeschooling father from Pennsylvania, "homeschooling was a natural extension of our belief in the family unit and our commitment to preserving the children's natural abilities to be creative, inventive problem-solvers and directors of their own learning." "Our life is geared toward self-sufficiency, self-reliance, and non-authoritarianism," writes a couple from West Virginia. "Also we want more and better education for our children than is expected in most schools in grades K–12." "We believe we can educate our children on our own better by allowing them to follow their own interests than by the mass education's methods of curriculum and schedule that provides for the convenience of the teacher rather than the needs of the learner," writes a mother of four from Idaho. "Another reason for our homeschooling is probably a selfish one. I like to be around my children and watch their growth and development. I do not want them away from home as many hours and days as are required by the public school." "We wanted to share the learning experience with our children," write the parents of five from Texas. "The school seemed to control our lives to the point where we didn't have time to do the things we felt were important." "Homeschooling fosters the innate joy of learning," write the parents of three from Arizona. "It avoids undesirable aspects of school socialization, such as grades, an emphasis on silent obedience, the equation of learning with work, and others. It returns strength to the family. And it allows greater interaction with the real world and with people of various ages and interests."

If any one person can be said to have fathered the modern homeschool movement, it's the late John Holt, innovative author of a stream of groundbreaking books about how children do (and do not) learn. Holt's *How Children Fail*, first published in 1964, was based on his classroom experiences as a fifth-grade teacher. Children fail to learn, Holt believed, because schools stifle their desire to investigate and explore, instilling instead a fear of failure, a sense of powerlessness, and a conviction that the fulfillment of their natural curiosity is less important than obeying the demands of their teacher. This was followed by the more upbeat *How Children Learn* (1966), a fascinating description of how young children—given sufficient freedom—teach themselves. A typical learning experience involved a class of first-graders who watched as Holt—armed with T square, ruler, and cutting knife—sat at the back of their classroom making small cardboard boxes of various dimensions. The kids, intrigued, soon set out to make boxes of their own. They did not have enough time, Holt regretted, to pursue the many mathematical possibilities inherent in box-making; their regular classroom teacher had other uses for their time. "However," wrote Holt, "in the short time that they were working [on the boxes], one little boy did a remarkable piece of work which in time might have led him and the class in directions I had never even thought of. Incidentally, he had been one of the more troublesome members of quite a troublesome class. After making a few boxes with open tops, he began to think about the problem of making a box with a closed top. He soon figured out what shape piece he had to cut out in order to do this. Then, looking at his closed box, he began to think of it as a house, and drew doors and some windows on it. But this wasn't a very interesting, or house-like-looking house...I didn't see him work on the problem, and don't know by what steps he managed it, but within a few days his teacher showed me a cardboard house with a peaked roof that he had cut out in one piece...A most extraordinary piece of work."

Holt initially hoped to apply his observations of children's learning methods to the classroom, thus improving the effectiveness of the schools. This hope was short-lived. The schools, Holt soon concluded, were unwilling to give children the freedom to learn in their own way. Instead they were intent on continuing to do what they had always done: "Teach them to Shut Up and Do What You're Told." The solution could only be found outside the system. Take the kids out of school and teach them—allow them to learn—at home.

Many homeschoolers find the very structure of the public schools—what John Taylor Gatto calls "the hidden curriculum of compulsory schooling"—to be inimical to effective learning. School, explains Gatto—who was designated the New York State Teacher of the Year in 1991—by virtue of the way in which it teaches, inculcates a train of damaging lessons that stifle intellectual and emotional development. The school, for example,

Books by John Holt

How Children Fail.
Perseus Press, 1995.

Based on his experiences as a teacher, Holt demonstrates how schools stifle children's natural curiosity, promote fear and intellectual dependency, and thwart real learning.

How Children Learn.
Perseus Press, 1995.

Descriptions of the many ways in which children learn effectively and independently when given the freedom to experiment and explore.

Instead of Education.
Delta/Seymour Lawrence, 1977.

Learning outside of school: alternative means of education using the resources available in neighborhoods and communities.

Learning All the Time.
Perseus Press, 1990.

How kids learn reading, writing, science, math, and music by interacting naturally with the world around them.

Teach Your Own: A Hopeful Path for Education.
Delta/Seymour Lawrence, 1981.

The hows and whys of homeschooling, with answers to common questions and concerns, and many descriptions of families teaching their own at home.

What Do I Do Monday?
Heinemann, 1995.

Many creative suggestions for implementing John Holt's theories with kids at home or in classrooms.

For materials by and about John Holt and his philosophy, see John Holt's Bookstore Catalog, Holt Associates, 2380 Massachusetts Ave., Suite 104, Cambridge, MA 02140-1226; (617) 864-3100; fax (617) 864-9235; e-mail: holtgws@erols.com; Web site: www.holtgws.com.

---

promotes confusion by exposing kids to arbitrary sequences of disconnected facts (dinosaurs in grade 3; the solar system in grade 4; electricity in grade 5) that prevent them from forming meaningful intellectual frameworks of their own. It encourages intellectual dependency, reinforcing the idea that, rather than seizing the initiative and thinking for themselves, good students wait to be told exactly what to do. It teaches, state professors Neil Postman and Charles Weingartner in *Teaching as a Subversive Activity*, that the voice of authority is more important than independent judgment; and that there is a single "Right Answer" to every question. This message, write Postman and Weingartner (see below), "is communicated quietly, insidiously, relentlessly, and effectively through the structure of the classroom: through the role of the teacher, the role of the student, the rules of the verbal game, the rights that are assigned, the arrangements made for communication, the 'doings' that are praised or censured. In other words, the medium is the message."

The End of Education: Redefining the Value of School.
Postman, Neil; Alfred A. Knopf, 1995.

The underlying themes of modern education, writes Postman, are economic utility, consumerism, technological dependence, and multicultural separatism—none of which prepare students for the rapidly changing modern world. The book proposes a new philosophy of education and describes strategies for implementing it.

Teaching as a Subversive Activity.
Postman, Neil and Charles Weingartner; Dell, 1969.

A detailed description of a revolutionary approach to teaching and learning. Chapter titles include "Crap Detecting," "The Medium Is the Message, Of Course," "The Inquiry Method," and "What's Worth Knowing?"

Our three sons, now teenagers, have always been homeschooled. Our reasons for doing so were a mixed bag of the philosophical, the academic, the social, and the idiosyncratic. My husband, Randy, and I chose to homeschool because we felt that a large—and largely impersonal—institution is not the best place for children to acquire an education. We chose to homeschool to promote family closeness, to foster creativity and independent thinking, to allow the boys to learn in their

Music lessons—or lessons in anything—can be dangerous to us, for the weekly guilt can become addictive. We can come to believe that we deserve scorn, and that we really can profit from being told repeatedly how to do it, from being given "right" answers. Gradually we lose our child-like enthusiasm for music or tennis or roller-skating or tightrope walking and substitute instead an intense yearning to do it "right" for the teacher.

ELOISE RISTAD
A SOPRANO ON HER HEAD

own way at their own speed. We chose to homeschool so that the boys would ask their own questions, with the freedom to pursue their own individual interests. And finally, we chose to homeschool because we wanted to be nearby as they explored and investigated their world, watching, loving, and learning with them. Simply being there, available to share in your children's revelations and discoveries—what one parent calls the "Eureka!" moments of learning—is a priceless advantage in homeschooling.

When we first officially committed ourselves to home education in the fall of 1987, Joshua, our oldest son, was six; his younger brothers, Ethan and Caleb, respectively four and three. Our local school district was emphatically hostile to our decision; our friends and families, many of them parents of conventionally schooled children, ranged from the mildly skeptical to the downright disapproving; and even I—the parent who was at home full-time, facing the lion's share of the day-to-day teaching—was nervous. *Are we courting academic and psychological disaster? Would the boys be better off in a classroom? What if I don't have enough patience to do this? What if homeschooling restricts, rather than broadens, our children's future options? And—every parent's nightmare—will they all hate us for this when they grow up?*

As we moved further into the experience of homeschooling, however, these fears turned out to have a diametrical opposite. Now, looking back, I think: *What if we hadn't home-schooled?* I remember the Eureka! moments: Joshua, wide-eyed, discovering infinity ("So once you start counting you can just go on and on and on, forever!"); Ethan, sitting bolt upright in bed, suddenly zeroing in on the awful deficiences of Dr. Seuss ("That machine would *never work!* The pulleys aren't connected to anything!"); Caleb, practically overnight, mastering reading *("Listen to me! I can read!").*

Perhaps for any homeschooling parent the reasons for our educational choices become clearer in retrospect. My home-school journals—a collection of bulging cardboard-covered notebooks—are a growing record of just exactly why we home-school.

◆ January 3, 1988

Josh is writing a play: Hansel and Gretel. *He spent the morning inventing dialogue, devising stage sets, and making costumes for everybody, including a Gingerbread House outfit for himself, made from a paper bag with square windows for eyes, decorated with candy canes. Ethan is playing the part of Hansel; Caleb, Gretel; Randy, the Mean Stepmother who throws the kids out to wander in the forest; and me, the Wicked Witch. The Gingerbread House, in Josh's version, has a mind of its own and is going to help Hansel and Gretel shove the Wicked Witch into the oven.*

Randy brought retractable metal measuring tapes home for each of the boys last night. A huge success; they spent most of today measuring everything in sight, enthusiastically comparing, contrasting, and discussing the specifics of yards, feet, inches, and fractions of inches. Then poor Caleb broke his tape by pulling it out too far and yanking it right out of its case. He cried; Ethan tried to fix it for him and couldn't; then promised to share his tape measure with Caleb forever...

The heart of our homeschooling program throughout the boys' elementary school years was group reading. We read daily and extensively, covering an immense range of authors and topics—all with accompanying conversation, questions, discussions, and debates. Reading was inevitably an open-ended and multifaceted experience, leading into imaginative play, scientific experiments, related field trips, and expeditions to the library for additional information.

◆ February 20, 1988

Read two National Geographic picture books this morning, The Blue Whales *and* Creatures of the Night, *which—what with all the questions and discussion—took us nearly two hours. Ethan, practically on page one, stumped us all by demanding to know what keeps fish down. "Why don't they just float to the top?" We didn't figure it out, but discussed air bladders, density, deepwater fish, water pressure, and scuba divers (weighted).*

More questions: "How do whales keep from bumping into icebergs? From getting caught under the ice?" "Can you see whales and squids from a submarine? What kind of windows are in a submarine?" "Why do some people eat whales? What does whale taste like?" "Does glass float?" (Josh: "Sure! Think about messages in bottles!" Ethan: "What about a sheet of glass? Would a windowpane float?")

On bats: "Bats can't be the only mammals that fly. What about flying squirrels?" "Why aren't birds mammals?" "Do bats hibernate?" "Are there really vampire bats?"

On kiwis, who sniff out earthworms to eat: "What do you suppose earthworms smell like?" "Why are earthworms good for gardens?" (Ethan knew; he also explained to his brothers how earthworms eat and excrete.) "Why is it bad for worms and slugs to dry out in the sun?" "Are moray eels poisonous?" (Ethan: "No, just very powerful biters. They don't have fangs.")

And so on and on.

Tomorrow: a trip to the library to pursue the floating fish question.

◆ **March 18, 1988**

We visited an artist's workshop today. The artist, a neighbor, does book illustrations. She showed the boys her tools and samples of her work; explained what she does and how; and let them experiment with some of her pens and inks. The boys admired her drawings and peppered her with questions. Back home, they all sat around the porch table and started personal artist's sketchbooks. Ethan drew submarines; Caleb drew magical people; and Josh drew giraffes. They also wrote (and illustrated) a joint thank-you note for the visit.

Did homemade math workbooks—"Continental Magic Math"—based on the continents of the world. The boys identified each continent on the world map and drew pictures and/or solved math problems related to each. (If you have seven penguins, and two penguins dive into the ocean...) They then—giggling hysterically—invented a series of continental math problems of their own. (If there are ten headhunters in the Amazon jungle and an anaconda swallows six of them...) Along the way, we discussed and/or looked up Indian buffalo hunters, koala bears, penguins, the Great Wall of China, and the average length of an anaconda.

Read a stack of picture books, including a nonfiction history of ships titled Traveling by Sea Through the Ages *(one of Ethan's recent picks from the library). This generated lots of questions and conversation. We covered dugout canoes, coracles, the Phoenicians, the first anchors, Viking longships, galley slaves, carracks, caravels, and galleons, square versus lateen sails, clipper ships, steamboats, paddle wheelers, and scurvy.*

Josh developed a sore throat just before bedtime and was convinced he had scurvy. He demanded a lemon.

During the boys' elementary and middle school years, among our most frequently used materials were "home-written interactive workbooks" on a wide range of topics, multiple copies of which could be produced via copy machine or computer printer. These homemade booklets were specifically tailored to the boys' current interests, skill levels, and senses of humor, and generally included both basic background information and a range of related multidisciplinary projects and activities, plus generous space for writing and drawing. Using the books, the boys drew topic-related illustrations and cartoons, wrote stories and poems, designed scientific experiments, and did craft projects.

◆ **September 26, 1989**

It's Johnny Appleseed's birthday today, so we read apple-related picture books and did home-written interactive workbooks all about apples. We began with Adam and Eve's famous apple, reading both the story of the Garden of Eden in Catherine Marshall's Story Bible *and a modern article about what fruits were better suited to a Middle Eastern climate than apples (dates? bananas?). The boys drew elaborately patterned and colored coiled paper snakes. Then they learned the scientific name for apple (genus Malus) and we discussed the difference between scientific and common names, with many plant and animal examples, among them our own Homo sapiens. Read a picture-book version of the story of William Tell, calculated how long ago William Tell lived, identified Switzerland on the world map, and drew dramatic Tell illustrations. (Josh made a target picturing a boy with an enormous apple on his head, which the kids plan to use this afternoon while practicing with their bows and arrows.) Read the story of Atalanta's race and the distracting golden apples in D'Aulaire's* Book of Greek Myths, *and the boys invented and illustrated their own versions of the story: Josh's picture shows a triumphant Atalanta zooming past the prince in a rocket car. We discussed Isaac Newton's apple, located England on the world map, and read* Gravity Is a Mystery *by Franklyn Branley (in the Let's-Read-and-Find-Out Science Series).*

The boys looked at the "apples" of their eyes—the pupils—in the mirror, discussed pupil and iris and their functions. We did a few experiments, observing the pupil dilate and contract in response to dark and light. Caleb and Josh drew detailed pictures of their own eyes; Ethan—announcing that he'd had enough of human eyes—drew a rainbow dragon's eye. A rainbow dragon's iris, it turns out, consists of six concentric circles, sequentially colored red, orange, yellow, blue, green, and purple.

Read Johnny Appleseed by Aliki and the poem "Johnny Appleseed" in Stephen Vincent Benet's A Book of Americans, and the boys all drew pictures of Johnny, which they posted on the refrigerator. (They also tried wearing pots on their heads, which they deemed very uncomfortable.) Over lunch we read Miss Rumphius by Barbara Cooney (discussing similarities to Johnny Appleseed) and The Giving Tree by Shel Silverstein.

In the afternoon, we went for a long walk in the woods, which involved more discussion of trees. "How tall is an apple tree?" "What's the tallest tree in the world?" "How many apples do you get from just one apple tree?" "What do you call a baby tree?" "Why does it kill a tree when you cut off its bark?" "Where are the seeds of a pine tree?" "How do you tell if a cone is ripe?" The boys then made a collection of cones in all possible permutations, among them open, closed, and chewed by squirrels.

Kids' questions are the bedrock of homeschooling, and the process of helping them find answers to their questions is the essence of learning. Questions come fast and furious in the early years. In fact, there's nothing so likely to reveal the gaping holes in an adult education as a few hours spent in the company of the average curious kindergartner. How do squirrels find their buried nuts? Is there a North Pole on the moon? What's inside a television? How much does a blue whale weigh? How long ago did King Arthur live? What makes fireworks green?

It's the rare parent—unaided—who can provide all of the answers; and in any case, it's doubtful that we should even if we were capable. Our purpose, as teaching adults, is to show our children how to learn for themselves: how to propose and weigh alternatives, how to estimate, reason, research, and look things up. As kids grow older and increasingly independent, their questions gradually taper off. They have tools and techniques of their own now; rather than "What's the tallest tree in the world?," they'll ask "Hey, Mom! Where's *The Guinness Book of World Records?*"

◆ April 19, 1990

Ethan just discovered the third dimension. He was drawing at the dining room table; then suddenly started shouting "Mama! Mama! Come here quick!" I came quick and found that he'd figured out how to draw cubes. The cube discovery was followed very rapidly by three-dimensional rectangles, houses, barns, and containers of strawberry Jell-O; and then a three-dimensional can (cylinder). Ethan was simply beside himself with excitement. He tried to show Caleb how to do it, but Caleb insisted that he'd rather figure it out for himself.

◆ November 20, 1990

Josh began the morning by writing out a long list of questions that he wanted to have answered. It began:

1. *Can crocodiles roar?*
2. *If there is a devil, what does he look like?*
3. *If you could travel in a time machine to the time of the dinosaurs, would* Tyrannosaurus rex *eat you? Could you outrun him?*

And many many more. After dealing with these, as much as possible, we went to our project of the day: Water, using homemade interactive workbooks. We first read about the water cycle, after which the boys made "rain" over the kitchen stove using a pot of hot water and a pie plate full of ice cubes. We discussed and diagrammed the chemical structure of water molecules—"How is a molecule different from an atom?"—and read about cohesion among water molecules. Discussed how soap works. Josh: "So that's how soap cleans things! It breaks up that skin of molecules and dissolves the dirt!" Also discussed water-skimming insects and drew pictures of what would happen to a water skimmer with soapy feet. (Ethan: "He'd sink!")

We did several experiments to demonstrate the surface tension of water, variously using liquid soap, black pepper, and paper boats. We repeated all several times; the boys were fascinated. We discussed why things float and demonstrated floating/sinking with clay. The boys first sank balls of clay in a big bowl of water; then tried to turn their balls into a form that would float. All eventually came up with some kind of floating clay boat. (They enjoyed themselves to no end; this project was a definite success.) While making and testing their boats, we discussed Archimedes and his principle, Magellan's ship Trinidad and why it sank (overloaded with spices), and the Titanic and why it sank (lethal iceberg). The boys promptly overloaded their clay boats with various objects and sank them. Josh wrote a song about the sinking of the Titanic and taught his brothers to sing it, which all did, repeatedly...

◆ **April 19, 1991**

The anniversary (well, yesterday) of Paul Revere's famous ride. The boys all made Paul Revere–style punched-tin lanterns (project from Steven Caney's Kids' America), using giant metal juice cans. While they worked, I read them Longfellow's poem "Paul Revere's Ride" (the boys loved it; they said it gave them the shivers), "Concord Hymn" by Ralph Waldo Emerson, and the Jean Fritz biography And Then What Happened, Paul Revere?

Ethan painstakingly made wire handles for all the lanterns; we then equipped them with candles and took them outside to see if they were really windproof, as the book had said. (Conclusion: they need tops.)

Paul Revere questions: "How does cloth muffle the sounds of oars?" "When they put those lights in the Old North Church, wouldn't the British have seen them too?" "Is a transport the same as a man-o'-war?" "Was Boston the biggest city in the colonies? How big is Boston now?" "Was Paul Revere upset when his babies died? How many children would he have had if none of them had died? How big was his house?" "Why was it so important for Paul Revere to get those papers of John Hancock's? What was in them?" "Was Lexington the battle where the man crawled home across the lawn to die on his own doorstep?" "Was that the battle where the leader said 'Don't fire until you see the whites of their eyes'? What is the white part of your eye made of?" "Who did fire the first shot at the Battle of Lexington and Concord?"

Started reading Mr. Revere and I by Robert Lawson. It's the story of the Revolutionary War told from the point of view of Paul Revere's (Tory) horse.

This process of question and answer, exploration and investigation, is what learning is all about. In this mode, learning is unmistakable; the atmosphere fairly crackles with interest and discovery. Homeschooling nurtures such an atmosphere, giving the kids the freedom to satisfy their own curiosity—to spend an afternoon, if the fit takes them, collecting rocks, dissecting evergreen cones, and discussing the habits of squirrels. Homeschoolers can go with the flow. No one tears them away from their model rocket because it's time—right now!—to do math; and if they're enthralled by *The Borrowers, The Hobbit,* or *Hamlet,* they can curl up with the book and—uninterrupted—*read.*

I think, at a child's birth, if a mother could ask a fairy godmother to endow it with the most useful gift, that gift should be curiosity.

ELEANOR ROOSEVELT

The reverse holds true too: when interest is patently absent and your young learners are squirming miserably in their chairs, you can drop what you're doing, fast. A kid who doesn't want to learn something, won't. Period.

◆ April 10, 1990

Reading with Ethan and Caleb in Teach Your Child to Read in 100 Easy Lessons *(Siegfried Engelmann, Phyllis Haddox, and Elaine Bruner; Simon & Schuster, 1983). Caleb is clearly a sight reader; he reads rapidly, he seems to recognize practically everything; but he has trouble sounding out unfamiliar words. (Me: "That's what phonics is for, Caleb. You can use it to figure out words for yourself." Caleb: "I like it better when you just tell me.") Ethan, however, is a whole different kettle of fish. No matter how relaxed and low-key I try to make a reading session, for him it isn't. He is a bundle of fidgets. He twitches, wiggles, climbs up and down over the arm of the chair. Persist, one book tells me. Don't drop something just because your child finds it frustrating. Keep plugging. It's a necessary part of the learning process.*

Presuming, that is, that what you're doing really is a "learning process." Today Ethan, miserable, announced that he would rather kill himself than read one more word in that stupid book.

I dropped it like a hot brick.

Ethan spent the rest of the afternoon happily drawing pictures, carving candles into the shape of little people, building Lego spaceships, and playing outside with his brothers, constructing "Robin Hood houses" in the woods.

Education is a notoriously slippery term, and the way in which it is defined has profound implications for the conduct of any school—public, private, alternative, or home. Without such a definition in place, goals become vague and unsubstantial; programs, fragmented and inconsistent. What is education for? homeschooling parents must ask themselves. What constitutes a good education? Where are our goals here? What do we want for our children? What will our children find most valuable for themselves?

To me education is a leading out of what is already there in the pupil's soul. To Miss Mackay it is a putting in of something that is not there, and that is not what I call education. I call it intrusion.

MURIEL SPARK
THE PRIME OF MISS JEAN BRODIE

What is education then? If it doesn't help a human being to recognize that humanity is humanity, what is it for? So you can make a bigger salary than other people?

BEAH RICHARDS
I DREAM A WORLD

Since the turn of the century, views of what schools are for—and what constitutes a good education—have changed time and again. Is, for example, the primary role of education to generate competent workers to support a growing national economy? (Or, put another way, are you educating your children so that they can get good jobs?) Is it to furnish the young with the academic basics? To inculcate a battery of approved social skills, psychological traits, and moral beliefs? To integrate a diverse array of ethnic groups into the mainstream American culture? To preserve and promote multicultural heritages? To create patriotic democratic citizens?

Perhaps the most all-encompassing problem that public education faces is the inability of the system to answer that question: What is education for? This isn't for lack of answers, but the reverse: the public schools are beset with too many answers, too many definitions, too many conflicting demands. It is impossible, en masse, to reach a consensus. The definition of education—like the definition of happiness—is an individual construct, a highly personal call. No two educations, ultimately, are alike; all are as unique as the patterns of individual fingerprints. Furthermore, the bulk of each education consists not of what has been thrust upon us, but what we—motivated by interest, curiosity, or necessity—have chosen to acquire for ourselves. All of us, educationally speaking, are specialists; we pick and choose, interconnect and assemble, select what suits us from among the rich immensities of human knowledge. My own eccentric and ever-accumulating education is different from that of my husband; and our educations in turn are very different from those being built by our sons.

Such individuality doesn't preclude the necessity for a common academic ground. No education consists solely of a whimsical collection of temporary fascinations. Our definition of education involves a solid foundation in the academic basics, those subjects that give kids the necessary tools for moving independently into a lifetime of learning. We wanted our kids to develop a love of learning and the motivation to specialize—to take their academic know-how and run with it, using it to pursue their own interests in their own way. A true education is never static. Rather than a finite object to be acquired, like a sack of scholastic potatoes, it is an active process, a verb rather than a noun.

A good education should leave much to be desired.

ALAN GREGG

And finally, successful schooling demonstrates unmistakably that teachers aren't necessary. The ultimate test of homeschooling is the realization that you—the parent, the teacher—have been left behind in the dust. I know homeschooling works because Randy and I are now—mostly—obsolete. I know homeschooling works because Josh is independently reading his way through English literature; because Ethan is teaching himself Russian and computer programming; because Caleb, on his own, is learning ancient history, astronomy, and how to play the recorder.

Schoolmasters and parents exist to be grown out of.

JOHN WOLFENDEN

MOST COMMON REASONS FOR HOMESCHOOLING

1. **Academic concerns.** Dissatisfaction with the public schools is presently rampant. A host of studies documents declining public school academic performance: science and math scores of American students are poor in comparison to those of their peers in other developed countries; standardized test scores are dropping (average SAT verbal scores, for example, are down fifty-four points since the 1960s); and 25 percent of graduating high school seniors—according to the National Assessment of Educational Progress (NAEP)—are so deficient in basic reading skills that they can barely decipher their own diplomas. Teachers often don't do much better. Some studies indicate that as many as 60 percent of certified teachers are underprepared for their jobs; and the results of the first Massachusetts Teacher Test, administered in 1998, revealed—to national horror—that 59 percent of teacher candidates were unable to pass a basic literacy test. Such doleful statistics prompt many concerned parents to keep their kids at home, where individualized instruction, freedom to pursue personal interests in depth, and the ability to adapt to varied learning styles and paces all contribute to an enhanced educational experience.

2. **Religious convictions.** Many homeschoolers—over half of all homeschooling families, by some estimates—teach their children at home primarily for religious reasons. Often families find that the curricula and teaching materials used in the public schools are not in tune with their spiritual, philosophical, and ethical values and beliefs. In some cases, separation of church and state preclude the schools from espousing religious viewpoints; in others, established school policy oversets parental opinions. Massachusetts parents protesting material presented in school sex education programs, for example,

were told by the state supreme court that "parents have no right to tailor public school programs to meet their individual religious or moral preferences."

Christian homeschoolers constitute a united and vocal subset of the homeschooling community. The largest national homeschool group—the Home School Legal Defense Association (HSLDA)—is a conservative Christian organization under the direction of Michael Farris, lawyer, father of nine, and one-time cochairman of Pat Buchanan's presidential campaign. Many homeschool periodicals and educational resource suppliers provide information and materials specifically targeted toward Christian homeschoolers.

3.   Negative socialization. "The social life of most schools and classrooms," wrote John Holt in his 1981 defense of homeschooling, *Teach Your Own,* "is mean-spirited, status-oriented, competitive, and snobbish." This is the socialization we hoped to avoid by homeschooling: the world of classroom bullies and peer pressure, the world in which children are unmercifully teased for being different, the world in which students are punished for nonconformity. While such negatives are unpleasant, other aspects of the school social structure are dangerous. According to an article in the October 5, 1998, issue of *Newsweek,* the primary reason for homeschooling cited by Florida parents was "safety." School, these days, can be a scary place. Public school violence is chillingly widespread: the nightly news is peppered with stories of students attacking teachers or students attacking each other, often with fatal effect. Every day across the nation some 130,000 students bring weapons to school. Among teenagers, pregnancies are on the rise, as is the prevalence of sexually transmitted diseases. Drug and alcohol abuse are endemic. Many parents homeschool in part to protect their children from this entire range of negative social experiences.

4.   Political philosophies. A conviction that unites homeschoolers of many disparate persuasions is the belief that they themselves—not the state—are responsible for their children's education. Such parental responsibilities have been consistently undermined by the expanding jurisdiction of state social programs and educational systems. Many of these programs—among them the public education system—have praiseworthy intentions: certainly children should be protected from neglect and abuse, given appropriate medical care, provided with an adequate education. Unfortunately, government has a heavy hand, and governmental "protections" in practice too often become governmental restrictions. The availability of free public education, for example, should not mean that parents have lost the right to choose the time and manner in which their children are educated. Parents who chafe under such restrictions often choose to homeschool.

5.   **Other.** Other reasons for homeschooling are legion, as varied and individual as the homeschooling families themselves. Some families homeschool out of a desire for increased family interdependence and closeness; some have specific personal values or beliefs that they wish to pass on to their children; some wish to pursue an independent and self-sufficient lifestyle. Some have children with special needs who require intensive individual attention, or gifted children whose talents cannot be properly nourished by the mass education system. Some simply want more time with their kids than is possible in the heavily scheduled course of public school attendance. And some—like us—agree with Thomas Jefferson, who once said, "Never ask anyone to do for you what you can do for yourself."

RESOURCES

BOOKS ON HOME AND ALTERNATIVE EDUCATION

The Almanac of Education Choices: Private and Public Learning, Alternatives and Homeschooling.
Mintz, Jerry; Simon & Schuster, 1996.
Descriptions of over 6,000 alternative schools and educational programs, plus informational essays by alternative educators.

Alternatives in Education.
Hegener, Mark and Helen, eds.; Home Education Press, 1992.
Descriptions of the many educational alternatives available to those unhappy with the public schools.

The Art of Education.
Dobson, Linda; Holt Associates, 1997.
A convincing and inspiring argument for family-centered education. Dobson writes, "Our one-style-fits-all approach to education oppresses spirit."

The Assault on Parenthood: How Our Culture Undermines the Family.
Mack, Dana; Simon & Schuster, 1997.
An account of how government bureaucracies, child-care and educational professionals, and the media combine to erode parental influence and familial bonds, and how families are beginning to combat this trend through grass-roots movements such as home-schooling.

The Dan Riley School for a Girl: An Adventure in Home Schooling.
Riley, Dan; Houghton Mifflin, 1994.
A detailed description of the year the author—a high school English teacher—spent homeschooling his 13-year-old daughter, Gillian.

Deschooling Our Lives.
Hern, Matt, ed.; New Society Publishers, 1996.
Essays on innovative alternatives to the public education system by 26 authors, among them John Holt and John Taylor Gatto.

Dumbing Down Our Kids: Why American Children Feel Good About Themselves But Can't Read, Write, or Add.
Sykes, Charles J.; St. Martin's Griffin, 1996.
Anti-intellectualism, the "religion of self-esteem," and outcome-based education are among the targets in this critique of the public school establishment. Home-schooling is included in the chapter on "The Coming Educational Revolution."

Dumbing Us Down: The Hidden Curriculum of Compulsory Schooling.
Gatto, John; New Society Publishers, 1992.
A terse indictment of the insidious "hidden curriculum" of the public schools by an award-winning teacher. Gatto declares, "Mass schooling damages children."

Family Matters: Why Homeschooling Makes Sense.
Guterson, David; Harvest Books, 1993.
A thoughtful presentation of the pros, cons, and how-tos of homeschooling.

Freedom Challenge: African-American Homeschoolers.
Llewellyn, Grace, ed.; Lowry House, 1995.
Essays and interviews with black homeschooling families.
Lowry House
Box 1014
Eugene, OR 97440-1014
(503) 686-2315

The Graves of Academe.
Mitchell, Richard; Simon & Schuster, 1987.
A merciless attack on the inadequacies of the educational establishment, the teachers' colleges, and "The Great Dismal Swamp" of public education.

The Homeschooling Book of Answers.
Dobson, Linda, ed.; Prima Publishing, 1998.
Commonly asked questions about homeschooling answered by 39 very different and very opinionated experienced participants.

Insult to Intelligence.
Smith, Frank; Heinemann, 1991.
A protest against the "drill and kill" style of teaching still so prevalent in the public schools, and suggestions for wiser alternatives.

Should I Homeschool? How to Decide What's Right for You and Your Child.
Hamilton, Elizabeth and Dan; InterVarsity Press, 1997.
Help in making educational decisions for your family.
InterVarsity Press
Box 1400
Downers Grove, IL 60515
(800) 843-4587, X230
e-mail: jconnon@ivpress.com

Taking Charge Through Homeschooling: Personal and Political Empowerment.
Kaseman, M. Larry, and Susan D. Kaseman; Koshkonong Press, 1991.
A discussion of the greater implications of the homeschooling movement and the ways in which it leads to a clarification of political and social values.

Homeschool Magazines

The Drinking Gourd
Box 2557
Redmond, WA 98073
(206) 836-0336
e-mail: TDrnkngGrd@aol.com
A multicultural magazine of homeschooling information, reader letters, and resource reviews.
6 issues/$18

Eclectic Homeschool
Box 736
Bellevue, NE 68005-0736
e-mail: Clayvessel@aol.com
Web site: eho.org
An on-line Christian magazine including feature articles on homeschooling topics, resource suggestions, a college and career department for older homeschoolers, and discussion groups.
Print version: 6 issues/$15

Family Unschoolers Network (F.U.N.) News
1688 Belhaven Woods Ct.
Pasadena, MD 21122-3727
voice mail/fax (410) 360-7330
e-mail: FUNNews@MCImail.com
Web site: www.iqcweb.com/fun/
General information, personal experiences, and resource reviews targeted at "unschoolers."
4 issues/$8

Growing Without Schooling
Holt Associates
2380 Massachusetts Ave.
Suite 104
Cambridge, MA 02140-1226
(617) 864-3100
fax (617) 864-9235
e-mail: holtgws@erols.com
Web site: www.holtgws.com
Founded by educator John Holt and dedicated to his educational philosophy, GWS includes informational articles, interviews, news updates, reader letters, resource reviews, and a regional directory of homeschooling families.
6 issues/$25

Home Education Magazine
Box 1083
Tonasket, WA 98855-1083
(509) 486-1351
(800) 236-3278
fax (509) 486-2753
e-mail:
HEM@home-ed-magazine.com
Web site: www.home-ed-press.com
Published by longtime homeschoolers Mark and Helen Hegener, this bimonthly magazine includes feature articles on homeschooling issues and experiences, teaching how-tos, book and resource reviews, news updates, and national and regional directories of homeschooling organizations and support groups.
For new homeschoolers, HEM publishes a free 30-page booklet, "Homeschooling Information and Resource Guide."
6 issues/$24

Home School Headlines
650 Company Farm Rd.
Aspers, PA 17304
(717) 528-8850
fax (717) 528-8124
e-mail: homesh@cvn.net
Web site:
www.homeschoolheadlines.com
Free online magazine for Christian homeschoolers including feature articles on homeschooling issues and methods.
Print version: 4 issues/$12

Homefires: The Journal of Homeschooling
180 El Camino Real
Suite 10
Millbrae, CA 94030
(888) 4-HOME-ED
e-mail: editor@homefires.com
Web site: www.Homefires.com
Articles on educational philoso-

phy and learning styles, teaching suggestions, networking, and resources.

6 issues/$32.85

HomeSchool Dad Magazine
609 Starlight Dr.
Grand Junction, CO 81504
e-mail: hsd@acsol.net
Web site: www.acsol.net/hsd
Family learning activities, homeschooling projects, Internet adventures, news, and reader letters. They also publish "A Father's Guide" of advice and activities for homeschool dads.

6 issues/$18

The Link: A Homeschool Newspaper
587 N. Ventu Park Rd.
Suite F-911
Newbury Park, CA 91320
(805) 492-1373
fax (805) 493-9216
e-mail: hompaper@gte.net
Web site:
www.homeschoolnewslink.com
Free bimonthly newsletter including essays, news updates, resource suggestions and reviews, and reader letters.

The Moore Report International
Box 1
Camas, WA 98607
(360) 835-2736
fax (360) 835-5392
e-mail: moorefnd@pacifier.com
Web site:
www.moorefoundation.com
Newsletter of the Moore Foundation, a Christian organization established by Raymond and Dorothy Moore, the "grand-

parents" of the homeschooling movement.

6 issues/$12

Practical Homeschooling
Home Life
Box 1250
Fenton, MO 63026-1850
(800) 346-6322
fax (314) 343-7203
e-mail: PHSCustSvc@aol.com
Web site: www.home-school.com
Articles, lesson plans, product reviews, and personal homeschooling stories for Christian homeschoolers.

6 issues/$19.95

NATIONAL ORGANIZATIONS

Alliance for Parental Involvement in Education (AllPIE)
Box 59
East Chatham, NY 12060
(518) 392-6900
e-mail: allpie@taconic.net
Web site: www.croton.com/allpie/
A nonprofit organization that promotes parental involvement in all learning environments. The group publishes two newsletters and a book and resource catalog.

Alternative Education Resource Organization (AERO)
417 Roslyn Rd.
Roslyn Heights, NY 11577
(516) 621-2195 or (800) 769-4171
fax (516) 625-3257
e-mail: jmintz@igc.apc.org
Web site: www.edrev.org
Provides information on many different kinds of alternative education programs.

American Homeschool Association (AHA)
Box 1083
Tonasket, WA 98855
(509) 486-1351
e-mail: AHA@home-ed-magazine.com
Web site: www.home-ed-magazine.com/AHA/
The purpose of the AHA is to promote home education, provide information to the general public, and support those providing materials and services to homeschooling families.

National Challenged Homeschoolers (NATHHAN)
5383 Alpine Rd. SE
Olalla, WA 98359
(206) 857-4257
fax (206) 857-7764
e-mail: NathaNews@aol.com
The group publishes a newsletter of information and resources for families with children with special needs.

National Home Education Research Institute (NHERI)
Box 13939
Salem, OR 97309
(503) 364-1490
fax (503) 364-2827
e-mail: mail@nheri.org
Web site: www.nheri.org
A nonprofit Christian organization dedicated to accumulating statistics on the homeschooling population. NHERI publishes a number of books and information packets and a quarterly journal.

National Homeschool Association (NHA)
Box 290
Hartland, MI 48353-0290
(513) 772-9580
Web site: www.n-h-a.org
The NHA provides general information about homeschooling and maintains a referral service to help new homeschoolers connect with local contact persons and support groups. It publishes a quarterly newsletter.

Native American Homeschool Association
Box 979
Fries, VA 24330
Web site:
expage.com/page/nahomeschool
Information and support for American Indian homeschoolers. Annual membership fee, $25.

HOMESCHOOLING INFORMATION ON-LINE

A to Z Home's Cool
Web site: hometown.aol.com/anaise/homeschool/index.html
General information about homeschooling, chat groups, a message board for posting questions, and state-by-state links to support groups and legal information.

The Caron Family Homeschool Homepage
Web site:
members.mint.net/caronfam
FAQs, a homeschooling booklist, hints for finding homeschool materials, information about

homeschoolers in high school, and over 800 links to homeschool resources on the Web.

Education: K-12 Alternative: Homeschooling

Web site: dir.yahoo.com/Education/
k_12/Alternative/Home_Schooling
A long list of useful and informative links.

Finding Homeschool Support on the Internet

Web site:
www.geocities.com/Athens/8259
Homeschooling resources and how-tos, discussion forums, lists of support groups and other homeschooling organizations, and lesson plans.

Heather's Homeschooling Page

Web site:
www.madrone.com/home-ed.htm
Interesting acounts of one homeschool family's experiences, covering such topics as "Deciding to Homeschool," "Socialization," and "Unschooling."

Homeschool Central

Web site: homeschoolcentral.com
A Christian site providing advice for new homeschoolers, study resources, curricula and catalog listings, and regional support group information.

Homeschool Connection

Web site:
members.aol.com/hsconnect
General information for homeschoolers, including FAQs, a newsletter, and links to related sites.

Homeschool Knotwork

Web site:
homeschool.knotwork.com
Essays, lists of books and periodicals on homeschooling, information on legal issues, on-line schools and courses, activities, how-tos, and discussion forums.

The Homeschool Zone

Web site:
www.homeschoolzone.com
The site includes general information, resources, a newsletter, an events calendar, discussion groups, and lists of regional support groups and pen pals.

Homeschooling Answers

e-mail: HSAnswers@aol.com
An online information service for new and experienced homeschoolers.

Homeschooling Kids with Disabilities

Web site:
members.tripod.com/~Maaja
Information, a discussion center, and links to useful sites.

Homeschooling at the Mining Company

Web site:
homeschooling.miningco.com
A large and varied site including FAQs, links to many homeschool publications, essays, reading lists, information on legal issues, news updates, chat groups, and a regional support group list.

Islamic Educational and Muslim Homeschool Resources

Web site:
home.ici.net/~taadah/taadah.html
Information and support for Muslim homeschoolers.

Jon's Homeschool Resource Page

Web site:
www.midnightbeach.com/hs
Justifiably called *"the* homeschooling page," this is an immense and multifaceted site with many (rated) links. Included are essays, homeschooling how-tos, information on legal questions, support group lists, chat groups and discussion forums, and resources.

School Is Dead; Learn in Freedom

Web site: learninfreedom.org
Information and opinion on home-schooling topics, essays, resources, book lists, and quotations. A good source for information about homeschoolers and college.

The Teel Home Education Page

Web site:
www.teelfamily.com/education/
Homeschool activities listed by topic, resource reviews, and links to many related homeschool sites.

HOMESCHOOLING AND THE LAW, OR NOTES FROM THE UNDERGROUND

I heartily accept the motto, "That government is best which governs least"; and I should like to see it acted up to more rapidly and systematically.

HENRY DAVID THOREAU
CIVIL DISOBEDIENCE

Once the decision to homeschool is made, the first step for homeschoolers with children of school age is to become acquainted with the stipulations of state homeschooling laws and local regulations. Kids under (or over) legal school age are not subject to such laws and regulations, so don't leap into anything prematurely. Definitions of "school age" vary somewhat from state to state, generally beginning anywhere from age five to eight and extending through age sixteen to eighteen. Young Virginians, for example, must be enrolled in school by the age of five; Vermonters, by the age of seven; and Pennsylvanians, by the age of eight.

My homeschool journal began, inauspiciously enough, on Friday the thirteenth in November 1987. Josh, our oldest son, was a school-age six that year; Ethan, our second son, almost five; and Caleb, our youngest, just three. We were living in La Honda, California, a tiny town in the redwoods south of San Francisco, onetime home of Ken Kesey and the Grateful Dead, then the stomping ground of potters, schoolteachers, sheep farmers, artists, computer programmers, and physicists from the Stanford Linear Accelerator. We had a blue house, a brown van, two orange cats, and a goldfish. And we were criminals. We were homeschooling illegally.

The illegal homeschooling underground, circa 1987, was nerve-wracking territory. Early issues of such national home-schooling magazines as *Home Education Magazine* and *Growing Without Schooling* were filled with stories of legal struggle, accounts of parents hauled into court at the behest of angry school officials, tales of state threats (some carried out) to remove homeschooled children from their parents' custody and send them to foster homes, and ominous-sounding lists of "friendly lawyers"—ominous because, running your finger through their names, you suspected you might someday need one.

Today the legal aspects of homeschooling—though not always comfortable for the families involved—are at least increasingly well defined. Homeschooling is legal in all fifty states, from Alabama to Wyoming, though requirements vary widely among them, ranging from the comfortably permissive to the nitpickingly restrictive. Missouri homeschoolers, for example, are blessed with one of the least invasive laws in the nation, requiring only that parents maintain a "daily log" of each child's educational activities and a portfolio of samples of each child's academic work. The first is to be used only in the event of run-ins with the law, as evidence of ongoing education; the second doesn't need to be shown to anybody unless parents or children feel like it. Missouri homeschoolers do not even have to announce their educational intentions to the school authorities, though those worried about unexpected visits from the truant officer may wish to declare themselves just to eliminate potential annoyance.

On the opposite end of the scale, Pennsylvania homeschoolers must wrestle with a labyrinthine list of bureaucratic regulations, first filing an annual affidavit listing names and ages of the participating children and names and telephone numbers of the homeschool "supervisors" (usually Mom and Dad), along with an educational curriculum (by subject area) and an up-to-date immunization record (or official exemption) for each kid. Subjects to be taught are precisely specified, including English, mathematics, science, geography, history (state, U.S., and world), health, physical education, art, music, and—at both elementary and secondary school levels—"safety education, including regular and continuous instruction in the dangers and preventions of fires." (Optional: biology, chemistry, economics, trigonometry, and foreign languages.) The long-suffering supervisors must maintain a detailed portfolio of all materials used and student work completed; this portfolio must be evaluated and "graded" annually by an approved teacher or administrator. Standardized tests must be taken in grades 3, 5, and 8. If none of the above meets with the evaluator's approval, you may not be able to continue homeschooling. And if any of your children turn out to need special education services or to be gifted and/or talented, your program will need to be approved by a certified special education teacher or a licensed clinical or certified school psychologist.

It's not only the homeschooled kids who are under scrutiny here; often state law turns its chilly eye upon the qualifications of homeschooling parents as well. From the point of view of educational officialdom, the ideal home instructor is a state-certified teacher; if you happen to be one, your credentials will cut a lot of red tape. Some states require that the teaching parent have a high school diploma or its equivalent; others require some college background or a completed bachelor's degree. Parents can teach their kids in North Dakota if they possess either a teacher's certificate, a four-year college degree, or evidence of a passing grade on the National Teacher's Exam (NTE). They can also homeschool with nothing more than a high school diploma, but in such case they must be monitored by a state-certified teacher. Minnesota, whose Compulsory School Attendance Law states—in somewhat two-faced fashion—"The parent of a child is primarily responsible for assuring that the child acquires knowledge and skills that are essential for effective citizenship," offers a similar array of qualification possibilities: you can be a certified teacher or a teacher in an accredited private or parochial school; you can be supervised by a certified teacher; you can pass a teacher competency exam on your own; you can have a bachelor's degree; or—one senses legislative despair here—you can simply be the parent of the homeschooled children involved. Parents in Tennessee can homeschool children through grade 8 with a high school diploma; to homeschool their high school students, they need a bachelor's degree. Massachusetts ostensibly has no formal parental qualification requirements, but this may vary from school district to school district, since homeschooling approval is the prerogative of local superintendents and/or school boards.

In our California county in 1987, there were only three accepted roads to homeschooling. Legally, we could have participated in an "independent study" program under the direction of the local public school, using public school textbooks and following the public school curriculum, with weekly monitoring by a public school teacher. Or one or both of us—the homeschooling parents—could have acquired a California teaching certificate. Or we could have established a formal private school at home (student body: three). We had failed, for one reason or another, to do any of these. The first choice we wrote off almost immediately: "independent study" clearly wasn't all that independent, and our plans for home education did not involve reproducing a public school classroom in our living room. The second proved to be a remote option: Randy, my husband, and I, both with college-level teaching experience and Ph.D.s in cell biology, still needed over two years of education courses—including classes in sex and drug counseling and a stint of student teaching—to qualify for California certification. Choice number three—declaring our home a private school—looked the most appealing. The mandatory application form, however—when it finally arrived—quickly showed us to be deficient in fire escapes, refrigerator square footage, and protective fences. Now, not only were we educationally weird, but—barely months into homeschooling—we were delinquents. We were dropouts. We were officially underground.

From my homeschool journal:

◆ **December 10, 1987**

Still no sign of our requested private school affidavit; perhaps we've been lost in the bureaucratic shuffle. There was an article in the local paper today on homeschooling. "In California," writes the author, "all children must be enrolled in school, but some homeschooling parents get around that requirement by declaring themselves private schools. According to Al Dixon, the administrator of State and Community Schools for the Santa Cruz County Office of Education, between 15 and 20 of the county's 60 declared private schools have five or fewer kids. He is quick to note that this practice is of questionable legality, but says a lack of state resources makes it difficult to monitor private schools closely."

Santa Cruz County, rumor has it, is much more open to homeschooling than San Matteo County. Our superintendent—I talked to him—was vehemently negative.

◆ January 12, 1988

Started morning by reading a picture book called Oil Rigs and Tankers, *which generated lots of questions and discussion. "What's a derrick?" "Where are the diamonds on the drill bit?" "What's oil used for besides making gasoline?" "What's porous? How can a rock be porous?" We talked about crude oil versus refined oil, the process of chemical fractionation, and oil spills in the ocean and why they are damaging. I told the boys about research on oil-eating bacteria. Ethan has a better idea: he plans to invent a machine with a giant vacuum cleaner attached to an enormous tank, to be used for sucking up and storing spilled oil.*

After lunch, we collected Randy and went to a play: a Children's Theatre production of The Emperor's New Clothes, *which was perfectly delightful. Josh and Ethan loved it, but Caleb had a hard time sitting still; Randy and I put him between us and kept plying him with crayons and stuffing him with licorice.*

Met another homeschooling family at the play; they're from San Jose and have two elementary school–aged boys. Unlike us, they are homeschooling legally, having managed to register as a private school. (Their school district, they tell us, is quite support-ive of homeschooling. Maybe we should move to San Jose.) They recommend that we join the Home School Legal Defense Association (HSLDA), which—for an annual fee—pledges to defend members who run afoul of the law. I'd already looked into this: it's a conservative Christian organization whose members are primarily homeschooling for religious reasons. I can't see that it would be much help to a pair of skeptical scientists.

◆ January 21, 1988

An official from the county Department of Education called today. He—surprisingly—is supportive of homeschooling. While homeschooling is still legally a gray area in California, he feels that restrictions should be challenged and pressure brought to bear on the local school board to establish flexible independent study

guidelines. The best way for us to get around the county regula-
tions, he suggests, is to register the boys in an out-of-state private
school that supports homeschoolers (provided we get a statement
proving that the school is legitimate in its own home state). Or we
can just do nothing. The worst that can happen to us, says the sup-
portive official, is that the school district will come after us and
we'll get a $100 fine for truancy, which we can protest, and then,
if need be, we can take them to court.

So we're going to do nothing. After all, we've been criminals
for months now and I'm getting used to it.

The out-of-state private school option is favored by many
homeschooling families. Such "umbrella schools" register
homeschoolers as students under home study programs that
provide varying amounts of guidance depending on parental
requests. Examples include the Clonlara School in Ann Arbor,
Michigan, the Oak Meadow School in Putney, Vermont, and
the Upattinas School in Glenmore, Pennsylvania (for addresses,
see page 115). If your home state is willing to recognize such
institutions as viable alternatives to public schooling, you may
be legally home free. Unfortunately, such recognition is not
always forthcoming.

In the summer of 1990, we moved to Massachusetts and set
out once again—Randy and I were both well brought up—to
right ourselves in the eyes of the law. We called several school
districts and spoke to assorted school superintendents, which
soon underlined the problems inherent in leaving homeschoolers to the mercies of local whim: superintendents ranged from
the encouragingly delightful to the off-puttingly autocratic.

◆ **July 4, 1990**

Spent most of last week calling school superintendents, in
preparation for our move to Massachusetts. The first—a Mr.
Turner, a lovely man—was very tolerant and laid-back about
homeschooling. There are several homeschooling families in his

district, he told me, and all are doing well. All we need to do, he continued, is to make sure that we're properly covered so that there can be no objections from the state: he needs a general summary of our curriculum and a resource list. "Make sure you include physical education," said Mr. Turner. "What kinds of things do other homeschoolers in your district do for physical education?" I asked. "Just talk about running games or something," said Mr. Turner. I love Mr. Turner. We then discussed standardized testing, which he feels should be at the discretion of the parents; if we would like to have the boys tested, however, we are welcome to have it done at the public school. He hoped Randy and I would settle in his school district and he invited us to come meet him after we move.

Superintendent number two—a Ms. Perkins—was black night to Mr. Turner's sunny day. To date, she had had only one homeschooler in her district, who, as of September, would be returning—a sadder, but wiser, student—to public school. Ms. Perkins requires extensive curriculum descriptions and detailed weekly lesson plans. She reserves the right to visit the homeschooling home periodically to make sure that we're performing properly. (If not, our homeschool approval will be terminated.) She insists upon annual standardized achievement tests, to be administered at the public school by a public school official. She was unwilling to discuss, negotiate, or compromise upon any point. She demanded my name, address, and telephone number, told me to get my paperwork in on time, and hung up.

Superintendent number three was too busy to talk to me; his secretary passed me on to an underling who had never heard of homeschooling and didn't think it was possible in his district.

◆ July 30, 1990

We've finally zeroed in on an affordable house within reach of Randy's job, which—unfortunately—puts it out of the jurisdiction of the wonderful Mr. Turner, for whom I would have been willing to live in a chicken coop. Our future school district has just sent me their required "Home Instruction Alternative Approval Form." One of these must be completed for each child. I am asked to list the name and age of each kid, and then to attach: (1) Annex A, describing my anticipated daily and weekly instructional schedule—"the times which would ordinarily be devoted to those aspects of the child's instructional program which depart from what would ordinarily be possible at home if the youngster were attending school during the day"; (2) Annex B, divulging full information about the parent(s) giving the home instruction, including name, colleges attended, degrees received, college major and minor, type of certification (if any), current work and work history, and at least three references; (3) Annex C, describing the place in which the instruction will take place and any other places which will be major sites for instruction; and (4) Annex D, an outline of our proposed instructional curriculum, listing goals and resources to be used for teaching reading, language, mathematics, physical education, science, social studies, music, and art. "Please," says the form, "complete Annex D with some thoroughness."

There's a question at the very end—"May public school supervisors visit your home at any reasonable time to observe your child's instructional progress?"—to which I have answered "No."

◆ **December 12, 1990**

We have been observed.

Not by the school district, which—other than a two-line letter saying that our home school application was received—has benignly ignored us, but by a newspaper reporter. He spent the entire morning with us, observing the operation of a homeschool. We were wonderful. We had cocoa and homemade blueberry muffins. We had stacks of library books in the living room, art projects on the refrigerator, the kids' nature collection on the dining-room hearth, and the world map posted on the wall (with the huge tear in the middle, where Caleb poked through it with a stick, sneakily mended). The boys were enthusiastic, articulate, brilliant, and cooperative, which was nice for their mother, who knows their occasional darker sides. Our day's topic was chemistry, using a trio of homemade workbooks. First we defined the atom (and took turns playing the parts of subatomic particles in "human atoms," the boys variously being protons, neutrons, and very excitable electrons). I told the kids that 65 million atoms lined up equals a quarter of an inch; the boys measured $\frac{1}{4}$ inch with their rulers, named the number, and wrote out "65 million" in numerals. Defined element and compound; read King Midas and the Golden Touch (gold is an element) and explained the meaning of Sherlock Holmes's trademark saying "Elementary, my dear Watson."

Made aluminum-foil boats full of sugar and baked them in the oven, thus demonstrating that sugar is a compound (baked, it turns into a black mass of carbon). Set up an experiment to prove that water is a compound: electrolysis, using pencils (graphite rods), a six-volt battery, and bell wire. Bubbles of hydrogen or oxygen accumulated at the cathode or anode; the boys figured out which was which. Reviewed the chemical formula for water.

We then talked about oxygen and oxidation; defined burning. Performed an experiment (with candle, pie plate of water, and Mason jar) to demonstrate that burning requires oxygen. Josh figured out why the water rose up in the jar as the candle went out: "The candle has used up all the oxygen so the water takes up the oxygen's space in the jar!" Right on.

The boys bubbled with questions throughout, and talked about past projects: Ethan discussed pH; Josh told stories about Archimedes; Caleb talked about his current favorite book, The Berenstain Bears' Science Fair.

The reporter wanted to know whether or not homeschoolers resented paying school taxes; I said school funding was a complex question, but supporting a free public education system is a joint investment in our national future, and as such is our joint responsibility. (Besides, people with kids in private and parochial schools, people with grown children, and people with no kids at all, all pay school taxes.) He also asked about socialization and about the chances of homeschoolers getting into college. Then he ate another blueberry muffin and left.

The boys and I, exhausted by academic perfection, went to the movies.

The kids are very excited about seeing their pictures in the newspaper.

I hope our district superintendent sees it. Perhaps this will count as an "on-site inspection."

◆ **January 23, 1991**

The school district has just approved our 1990–1991 home-schooling curriculum. They are sorry for the delay. They forgot about us.

◆ **May 4, 1991**

We've just received a letter from the local elementary school principal. "As you know," it begins, "testing to assess your child's academic progress should be an important part of his/her home-schooling program. To facilitate collecting this information, we have arranged a testing period for the children who are currently being educated at home." Josh and Ethan are both scheduled for tests at the end of the month.

I've just fired back a letter saying that Randy and I don't feel that standardized tests are optimal measures for assessing the effectiveness of homeschooling and suggesting that we get together to discuss alternatives.

◆ **July 8, 1991**

Randy and I and the boys went to the elementary school today to meet the principal and to discuss our proposed methods of progress assessment and our next year's curriculum. I, perennially nervous, was geared up for difficulties, criticisms, veiled threats, and outright intimidation. Nothing could have been farther from *the truth. The principal was kindhearted, soft-spoken, friendly, and wore blue jeans. He shook hands with all the boys, which impressed them, and asked them what they liked to do in homeschool, which they practically fell over themselves to answer. Science experiments! Painting! Josh described the plot of* Black Beauty; *and all three discussed their recent history play,* The Story of the Revolution, *in which all play multiple parts. (Josh does everyone from King George III to Thomas Jefferson; Ethan plays Paul Revere and David Bushnell, builder of the submarine* The Turtle; *and Caleb plays Benedict Arnold and gets to hang the lanterns in the Old North Church.)*

Then the kids went out to investigate the school playground, and the adults had a comfortable conversation about educational resources, approaches, problems, and the like. The principal is happy with our evaluation process and our curriculum; said he'd appreciate updates on our progress from time to time; and said to call if we had any difficulties or anything we'd like to talk over. He has two children of his own (aged two and three). He is thinking of homeschooling.

While I know many homeschoolers who have had various disagreements with the public schools—over everything from curriculum content to testing requirements to permission to play on the school basketball team—I also know many homeschoolers these days who seem to have reasonably pleasant (or benignly neglectful) relationships with their local districts. I personally don't know anybody who has ever been hauled into court for perceived educational peccadillos, but the possibility—though increasingly slight—is there. In 1981, for example, the Texas Education Agency (TEA) decreed that homeschools, to date categorized and regulated as private schools, were *not* private schools, and thus could no longer be considered an acceptable form of education under state law. The TEA then proceeded to prosecute some 150 homeschooling families for failure to comply with the state compulsory school law. In

1985, the homeschoolers fought back: several homeschooling families, led by Gary and Cheryl Leeper, filed suit against the Arlington, Texas, school district and all other Texas school districts, asking for a court ruling stating that home-schools were indeed private schools. Despite repeated judgments in favor of the homeschooling families—the Texas Court of Appeals called the actions of the TEA "arbitrary, capricious and unreasonable"—the state continued to appeal. The case was finally settled by the state supreme court in 1994; Texas homeschools were once again private schools, and their students officially exempt from the compulsory attendance law.

Most confrontations between homeschoolers and the education establishment are less sweeping. Cindy Wade, homeschooling mother of two from East Wallingford, Vermont, answered her door in December 1996 to the town sheriff, armed with a truancy notice: a disgruntled official in the homeschooling division of the Department of Education had reported her failure to have her home study program formally approved by the state. "I gave the sheriff a cup of coffee," Cindy recalls, "and introduced him to my kids, and then we had a long talk about all the problems with the public schools. After he left, I called the district superintendent and our local school principal and explained my views: that parents, not school officials, have the responsibility for children's education. I also pointed out that if they decided to take us to court, it was going to cost the school district an awful lot of money. They decided to leave us alone."

How common are such problems? In general, while there are certainly obstructive public school officials out there, legal run-ins are rarer than they used to be. The Home School Legal Defense Association claims that some 2,500 families each year come to them for legal aid and advice. Only about 3 percent of these cases, however, develop into full-blown lawsuits. The majority of these—instigated by state or local school officials—

accuse parents of failing to meet state-required educational standards. If worse comes to legal worst, most (but not all; there are no guarantees) court decisions turn out favorably for homeschoolers. The fundamental rights of the homeschooling community are protected by a pair of Supreme Court decisions handed down in the 1920s. The first, *Pierce v. the Society of Sisters,* originated with an ill-considered Oregon statute that flatly abolished private schools, on the grounds that unless children all attended uniform public schools, they might be susceptible to various "undesirable ideas" communicated by their parents. Oregon private schools—among them a battery of parochial schools and at least one faultlessly patriotic military academy—rose up in arms; the resultant federal decision overturned the statute, ruling that while the state could compel the education of children, it could not require all children to be educated in the same place in the same way. A similar case, *Farrington v. Tokushige,* surfaced in Hawaii, when public officials attempted to force all private schools to adopt the public school curriculum. Protest ensued; again the Supreme Court ruled that the state could not impose a uniform system of education on all its citizens.

While the national stage has thus been set for freedom of educational choice, plenty of room remains for restrictive maneuvering on the part of the state. The current call for the establishment of national education standards under the 1994 Educate America Act (Goals 2000)—ostensibly a praiseworthy attempt to "ensure that all students learn to use their minds well, so they may be prepared for national citizenship, further learning, and productive employment in our nation's modern economy"—is a continued push for a uniform education for all. While the ultimate control of public education rests in the hands of the individual states, eligibility for forthcoming federal aid money will depend on each state's compliance with these national standards, as judged by student performance on nationally approved tests.

So far, we do not seem appalled at the prospect of exactly the same kind of education being applied to all the school children from the Atlantic to the Pacific, but there is an uneasiness in the air, a realization that the individual is growing less easy to find; an idea, perhaps, of what standardization might become when the units are not machines, but human beings.

EDITH HAMILTON
CLASSICAL SCHOLAR AND EDUCATOR

Since each state has its own way of dealing with the legalities of homeschooling, relationships between homeschoolers and the authorities can vary greatly from place to place. Generally, homeschool legislation falls into five basic categories: *Homeschool statute states* have passed laws that define and regulate homeschooling, sometimes very specifically and very strictly. Thirty-four states presently have passed such legislation, including Missouri and Pennsylvania. *Private school statue states* have either specifically deemed homeschools to be private schools or have defined *private school* in such a fashion that a homeschool, willy-nilly, is one. Homeschools are thus subject to the same regulations and restrictions imposed upon private schools, which vary again markedly from state to state. Ten states presently deal with homeschooling in this fashion, among them Alaska, California, and Texas. Three states—Connecticut, Idaho, and New Jersey—are *equivalent-instruction states*, which means that homeschoolers can do whatever they want, *provided* they teach the same subjects that are taught at their children's grade levels in the public schools. Two states—Massachusetts and Rhode Island—are *approved-instruction states*, which means that curriculum approval and evaluation requirements are in the hands of the local school district; this, depending on the people involved, can be pleasant and easy or stressful and difficult. One highly enlightened state—Oklahoma—has declared that homeschooling is a *constitutional right*; that is, the right of parents to teach their children at home is guaranteed in the state constitution.

The most direct source for discovering the ins and outs of local homeschooling laws is straight from the horse's mouth: you can read the law for yourself. Go to the public library and ask for a copy of your state's education code. This is generally long, convoluted, and written in the pompous lingo favored by lawyers and politicians, but it's the definitive text and worth reading. Next best is a homeschool support group. Such groups are generally filled with people who have considerable personal experience in dealing with the law; and local and state homeschool organizations often make it their business to monitor the homeschool legal climate and keep their members informed of changes, debates, and proposed legislation.

Local school districts or state Departments of Education may (or may not) provide accurate legal information. In Vermont, where homeschooling approval is meted out at the state level, the Department of Education offers a large and useful packet of materials for new homeschoolers, including an explanation of state-sanctioned requirements, all necessary legal forms, addresses of support groups, and even a list of good places to take your kids on field trips. In some states, however, school officials may be unfamiliar with the letter of the law— or they may have their own interpretations of the regulations, which may or may not be correct. When in doubt, it's best to gather information from several sources.

An alternative to all these legal complexities is what is politely called "noncompliance," which falls into two basic patterns: private, in which you don't obey the law but don't tell anybody what you're doing; and public, in which you not only don't obey the law, you flaunt your decision in public, thus courageously standing up for your principles. Public noncompliance carries more risks than private, since those who practice it are visible and hence more open to prosecution, litigation, and penalties. Noncompliance is favored by families who live in particularly difficult legal climates or whose personal philosophies conflict with homeschooling laws in general. New Hampshire passed a markedly restrictive homeschooling law in 1990; the New Hampshire Department of Education now estimates that at least half of state homeschoolers are noncompliant.

Some homeschool support groups and factions—notably those with a fundamentalist Christian base—are adamantly opposed to such civil disobedience, arguing that a lack of respect for authority jeopardizes the homeschooling movement in general. Debra Bell in *The Ultimate Guide to Homeschooling* writes: "Responsibly complying with the homeschool regulations governing your state, even those you do not agree with, will engender respect for the homeschooling movement at large." Well, maybe—but whose respect? And for what? A decision to homeschool is in many ways not only an educational but a political statement. Should the state dictate the way in which our children are educated? Should the opinions of the school system take precedence over the opinions of the parents?

And—if the answer to these last is a resounding "no"— what effect will a parental decision to flout the law have on our children? Will they grow up to question authority? Will they be rebels, ornery independent thinkers, out-of-step followers of different drummers?

Maybe. If we're lucky.

Here's one answer:

◆ **September 1, 1997**

Josh, Ethan, Caleb: Help. Please write an essay answering the following questions:

In your opinion, should homeschoolers comply with state laws and regulations concerning homeschooling, even if they disagree with the premises behind them?

Which is more important: to obey the agreed-upon laws of the state or to pursue a course that you personally believe is right?

Socrates and Thoreau Put on the Gloves
BY JOSH RUPP, AGE 16

In Plato's *Crito,* Crito, a friend of Socrates, visits the philosopher in his cell, where he is under a sentence of death for offenses against the laws of Athens. Crito implores Socrates to accept his offer to smuggle him out of jail and help him escape from the city. In reply, Socrates, implacably smug logician that he was, made the legendary argument that is the theme of *Crito:* He (Socrates) could not leave without the permission of the Athenians because, as a subject of the state, he has no right to go over the heads of the state. Even though he thought the state was doing him a wrong, he still had no right to break the law just because he personally felt that it was unjust. To overturn the laws of a state, no matter what your motivation, means that those laws have no power, and if so, the state itself would be powerless and would soon be destroyed. Since Socrates was a loyal citizen of the state, he could not allow that to happen. For a state to have any legitimacy, he insisted, its citizens must abide by its laws, both those laws they agree with and those they don't.

Socrates, always willing to put his money where his mouth was, chose to remain in Athens, and soon after was executed by the state. This incident remains a thorn in the side of those supporting the principle of civil disobedience. The fundamental and austere arguments of Socrates are at a stand-off with the argument that each individual must follow the dictates of his own conscience. On the other hand, those who subscribe to civil disobedience would argue that you *cannot* obey (or break) an unjust law.

The American government insists upon mandatory school attendance, and the public school thus has the power to regulate American education. Counter to this regulation, many families choose to educate their children at home. Over time, the government has grudgingly allowed that people have the right to do this. Some states don't interfere with these families' educational decisions at all, some interfere moderately, and some are extremely restrictive. That's why it's called "home *school,*" the logic clearly runs: people are "schooling" at home. This is seen as a formal process, and homeschoolers are expected to adhere to that school-like process or—depending on the state they live in—to desist from homeschooling entirely. Socrates would appreciate that logic. After all, if the state is to have any validity, you must adhere to its laws and abide by its educational system.

For any political system to succeed, a degree of social conformity is necessary. Otherwise, the system falls apart. If the individual decision takes precedence over the state, then there is no state. As such, just doing whatever you want in the educational field poses an actual threat to the concept of organized society. This is a difficult problem for those who wish to educate their children against the laws of the state. The decision to educate your children at home, in the way you deem fit, no matter how small and insignificant a decision it may appear from a social perspective, still constitutes civil disobedience. Civil disobedience by definition is contrary to the authority of the state. In that the ability of the country to educate children in the way that it feels necessary is an act of governmental control, home education against the will of the country is an act of revolution. Although homeschooling may appear to be a small and domestic decision, it is actually a threat against the stability and control of the nation.

So the gauntlet has been thrown. Civil disobedience versus the legitimacy of the state. The issue continues to come up and there is no solution for it but to wait for Socrates and Henry David Thoreau to put on the gloves, emerge from the mists of time, and battle it out.

RESOURCES

INFORMATION ON LEGAL AND RELATED ISSUES

Compelling Belief: The Culture of American Schooling.
Arons, Stephen; McGraw-Hill, 1983.

Home Education: Rights and Reasons.
Whitehead, John W., and Alexis Irene Crow; Crossway Books, 1993.

"On Jumping Through Hoops." *Home Education Magazine, May/June 1992.*
Hegener, Helen.
The May/June issue of *Home Education Magazine* includes several articles of interest, grouped under the heading "Perspectives on the Law."
Back issues, $4.50
Home Education Magazine
Box 1083
Tonasket, WA 98855
(800) 236-3278

e-mail:
HEM@home-ed-magazine.com
Web site:
www.home-ed-magazine.com

School Rights: A Parent's Legal Handbook and Action Guide.
Condon, Thomas, and Patricia Wolff; MacMillan General Reference, 1996.

Sources for Legal Aid

Home School Legal Defense Association (HSLDA)
Box 3000
Purcellville, VA 20134
(504) 338-5600
Web site: www.hslda.org
A national organization of home-schoolers with a conservative Christian political agenda. For an annual family membership fee of $100, the HSLDA offers legal advice and—in a limited sense—legal "insurance" to homeschooling families. The organization publishes a bimonthly newsletter.

National Association for the Legal Support of Alternative Schools (NALSAS)
Box 2823
Santa Fe, NM 87501
(505) 471-6928
An information and service organization that surveys legal issues surrounding alternative education and homeschooling. An annual membership costs $35, which includes a subscription to their quarterly newsletter.

The Rutherford Institute
Box 7482
Charlottesville, VA 22906
(804) 978-3888
A legal activist group with a somewhat unpredictable political agenda, headed by "reconstructionist Christian" John Whitehead. The Institute is pro-homeschooling.

State Laws and Regulations Summarized

For an overview of homeschooling laws and regulations, listed by state, see the American Home-school Association Web site at www.home-ed-magazine.com/AHA/HSIF/aha_lws.rgs.html or The Homeschool Connection, Inc., Web site: frontpage.inet-images.com/hsconnection

Alabama

In Alabama, homeschooled students must either be taught by a certified teacher or tutor or must register as a church school. Standardized tests are not required.
See Alabama Code 16-28-3.

Alaska

Students may be taught at home by a state-certified teacher, may be enrolled in a full-time approved correspondence course, may participate in a homeschool program approved by their local school board or official, or may register as a private or religious school. In some cases, standardized testing is required in grades 4, 6, and 8.

See Alaska Statutes 14-30.010 and 14.45-120(a).

Arizona

Students may be taught at home by their parents, who must instruct them in "at least the subjects of reading, grammar, mathematics, social studies, and science." No standardized tests are required.

See Arizona Rev. Statute 15-802 through 805 and 15-745.

Arkansas

Children may be taught at home by their parents, though special-needs students must be tutored or reviewed by a certified professional. Homeschool curricula are not subject to state approval. However, standardized tests are mandatory, and students with "unsatisfactory" test scores may be required to enroll in school.

See Arkansas Statute 6-18-201 and 6-15-501.

California

Children may be taught at home by a state-certified teacher, may participate in an independent-study program through the public school, or may register as a private school. Subjects to be taught are specified in great detail. Standardized tests are not required.

See California Education Code sections 48222, 48224, and 51745.

Colorado

Children may be taught at home by a state-certified teacher or by their parents, or they may be enrolled in a private school that permits independent study at home. A "non-public home-based education program" must include 172 annual days of instruction, averaging four "instructional contact hours" per day; the program must cover the "communication skills of reading, writing, and speaking, mathematics, history, civics, literature, science" and the Constitution of the United States. Standardized tests are required in grades 3, 5, 7, 9, and 11.

See Colorado Rev. Statutes 22-33-104 and 104.5.

Connecticut

Children may be taught at home by their parents provided they receive "equivalent instruction" to that offered in the public schools. An annual portfolio review is required.

See Connecticut General Statute 10-184.

Delaware

Homeschoolers must teach the same subjects that are taught in the public schools and must be in session 180 days per year. Standardized tests are not required, but "some means of demonstrating progress" is.

See Delaware Code 14-2702 through 2703.

Florida

Children may be taught in a "sequentially progressive" manner at home by their parents, who must maintain a portfolio of records and teaching materials. Evaluation by one of several different methods is required.

See Florida Statute 232.01.

Georgia

Children may be taught at home by their parents provided the primary instructor has a high school diploma or GED. A teacher who is not the child's parent must have a college degree. Homeschool programs must include instruction in reading, language arts, mathematics, social studies, and science, and must be in session 180 days per year, for at least 4.5 hours per day. Monthly attendance reports must be submitted to the local school superintendent. Standardized testing is required at intervals after grade 3, but parents are not required to submit test results to the local authorities.

See Official Code of Georgia 20-2-690.

Hawaii

Children may be taught at home by their parents under an "alternative education program" or by registering as a homeschool. They may also be taught at home by a tutor, who must have a college degree. Curriculum approval is not required; annual progress reports are. Standardized tests are required in grades 3, 6, 8, and 10.

See Hawaii Rev. Stat. 298–9.

Idaho

Children may be taught at home by their parents provided they receive instruction in the subjects "commonly and usually taught" in the public schools (English, math, reading, science, history, and civics). Standardized tests are not required but are available on a voluntary basis. The University of Idaho offers an accredited high school correspondence course.

See Idaho Code 33-202.

Illinois

Homeschools in Illinois are considered to be private schools. Such schools must be in session at least 176 days per year, for 5 hours per day; subjects taught must be equivalent to those taught in the public schools. Instruction must be in English. Standardized tests are not required.

See Illinois Rev. Statutes ch. 122, par. 26-1.

Indiana

Children may be taught at home provided they receive instruction "equivalent" to that provided by the public schools. Indiana homeschools are considered to be private schools. Parents are required to maintain attendance records. Standardized tests are not required.

See Indiana Statute 20-8.1-3-17 and 20-8.1-3-34.

Iowa

Homeschoolers must receive "competent private instruction," which means that the teaching parent must have a state teacher's certificate, or that the children must be enrolled in a supervisory homeschool assistance program through the public school or an "accredited nonpublic school." Standardized tests or some alternative method of evaluation are required. If children fail to make adequate progress, they are made to enroll in school.

See Iowa Code 299A.1.

Kansas

Several court decisions have ruled that a home may qualify as a "school." Standardized tests are not required.

See Kansas Statutes 72-111 through 72-1113.

Kentucky

A home may qualify as a "school." Parents must maintain attendance records. Standardized tests are not required.

See Kentucky Rev. Statutes 159-010 through 159.990.

Louisiana

Children may be taught at home by their parents provided that parent offers a curriculum equal in quality to that offered in the public schools. Homeschool programs must be approved annually by the local school district. Standardized tests or an evaluation by a certified teacher are required.

See Louisiana Rev. Statutes 17:221 (A) and 17.236.

Maine

Children must receive "equivalent instruction" to that offered by the public schools. The home study program must be reviewed by the local school board or school officials. Standardized testing or some other means of evaluation is required.

See Maine Rev. Statute 20A-5001A.

Maryland

Children may be taught at home by their parents provided they receive "regular, thorough instruction" in the subjects taught in the public schools. Families must either enroll in a state-approved nonpublic school, enroll in a religious school or organization, or participate in one to three annual portfolio reviews by district school officials. Standardized tests are not required.

See Annual Code of Maryland, ch. 22, 7-301 (a).

Massachusetts

Children may be taught at home provided the home study program is approved in advance by the local superintendent or school committee. Local school officials may require standardized testing or some other method of student evaluation.

See Massachusetts Gen. Laws 76-1.

Michigan

The home can be a school provided children are educated by means of "an organized educational program" that is appropriate to the child's age and abilities and covers specified academic subjects (reading, spelling, mathematics, science, history, civics, literature, writing, and English grammar). Standardized tests are not required.

See S.B. 679, Amendment A.

Minnesota

The primary homeschool instructor must have a state teacher's certificate, be supervised by a certified teacher, have passed the state teacher competency exam, possess a college degree, use an "accredited" educational program approved by the local school board, *or* comply with pupil testing requirements. Standardized tests are required only when a family chooses this last option; students who score below the 30th percentile must be evaluated for learning problems. Parents must submit an annual instructional calendar, quarterly progress reports, copies of teaching materials, and descriptions of their assessment methods to their local school superintendent. The superintendent may request an on-site visit to ensure homeschool compliance.

See Minnesota Statutes 120.101 and 127.20.

Mississippi

Parents must submit an annual "Certificate of Non-Public Enrollment" to their local school district. Standardized tests are not required.

See Mississippi Code 37-13-91.

Missouri

Homeschoolers must maintain attendance records and keep a portfolio of each student's work and records of progress evaluations. Children must receive at least 1,000 hours of instruction each year, of which 600 hours are spent teaching the "core" subjects: reading, language arts, mathematics, social studies, and science. Standardized tests are not required.

See Ann. Missouri Statutes 167-031 and 167.042.

Montana

Neither curriculum approval nor standardized tests are required.

See Montana Code 20-5-102 and 20-5-109.

Nebraska

Homes may qualify as "approved" private schools or as "exempt" private schools; in the latter case, parents must have sincere religious objections to public education and must file a notarized "Statement of Objection and Assurances" with the state. The primary instructor must possess a state teacher's certificate or meet local school board standards for exempt private schools. Standarized tests may be required, depending on the discretion of the local school board.

See Nebraska Rev. Statues 79-201, 79-1701, and 85-607.

Nevada

Homeschooled children must receive instruction "equivalent" to that offered in the public schools. The primary instructor must have a state teacher's certificate, must consult with a certified teacher, must use an approved correspondence course, or must obtain a waiver from the local school board. In some cases, standardized tests are required in grades 2, 3, 4, 7, and 8.

See Nevada Rev. Statute 392.070.

New Hampshire

Home education must consist of "planned and supervised instructional and related educational activities"; individual programs must be approved by the state Department of Education. Standardized tests or some other form of evaluation are required; children who do not make adequate progress are required to enroll in school.

See New Hampshire Rev. Statute 193:1 and 193-A.

New Jersey

Homeschooled children must receive "equivalent instruction" to that offered in the public schools. Parents do not need to notify their local school districts; however, they must maintain records, which must be made available to school officials upon request. Standardized tests are not required.

See New Jersey Statute 18A.38-25.

New Mexico

Parents must provide a "basic academic educational program." The primary instructor must possess a high school diploma or its equivalent. Standardized tests are required in grades 3, 5, and 8.

See New Mexico Statutes 22-1-2 and 21-1-2.1.

New York

Children taught at home must receive a "substantially equivalent" education from a "competent" teacher. Equivalency is determined by the local school board or designated school officials. Parents must provide their local superintendents with annual written notice of their intent to homeschool and must file, for each student, an "Individualized Home Instruction Plan" (IHIP). Quarterly progress reports and annual assessments, including standardized tests, are required.

See New York Education Laws 3204, 3205, 3210, and 3212.

North Carolina

A homeschool cannot include children from more than two families and must be taught by a parent or member of the household of one of the two families forming the "home." The primary instructor must have a high school diploma or equivalent. Homeschools must be in session for at least nine months annually, and parents must keep attendance records. Annual standardized tests are required.

See North Carolina Gen. Statutes 115C-378, 115C-547, and 115C-563 through 565.

North Dakota

Homeschoolers must file an annual notarized "statement of intent" with their local superintendent. The teaching parent must possess a state teacher's certificate, have a high school diploma and be supervised by a certified teacher, or pass the National Teacher Exam. Standardized tests are required in grades 3, 4, 6, 8, and 11.

See North Dakota Cent. Code 15-34.1-03 and 15-34.1-04.

Ohio

Home school programs must be approved by the local school board or designated school officials and must include instruction in language, reading, spelling, writing, geography, history of the United States and Ohio, government (national, state, and local), mathematics, science, health, physical education, fine arts (including music), first aid, safety, and fire prevention. The teaching parent must possess a high school diploma or its equivalent or be supervised by a person with a college degree. Standardized tests or some other form of evaluation are required.

See Ohio Rev. Code 3301-34-04, 3321.03, and 3321.04.

Oklahoma

Homeschools must be in session for the full term that the district public schools are in session and must include subjects typically taught in the public schools, including reading, writing, math, science, U.S. Constitution and citizenship, heath and safety, physical education, and conservation. Standardized tests are not required.

See Oklahoma Stat. Ann., Title 70, 10-105 (A) and (B).

Oregon

Parents must provide their local school superintendents with annual written notification of their intent to homeschool. Annual standardized tests are required. Children who do not show "satisfactory educational progress" may, at the district superintendent's discretion, be required to enroll in school.

See Oregon Rev. Statutes 339.010, 339.030, and 339.035.

Pennsylvania

Parents must file an annual notarized affidavit with their local school superintendent stating their intention to homeschool and outlining their proposed home education program. Children may be taught at home by a certified teacher or, under a "home education program," by a parent with a high school diploma or equivalent. Home education programs must be approved by the local school board or designated officials; courses to be taught are specified. Standardized tests are required in grades 3, 5, and 8, as well as an annual portfolio evaluation by a certified teacher or other professional.

See Pennsylvania Stat. Ann., Title 24, 13-1326 and 13-1327.

Rhode Island

Homeschool programs must be approved by the local school board or designated school officials. An evaluation may be required.

See Rhode Island Gen. Laws 16-19-1.

South Carolina

Homeschool programs must meet a number of specific requirements and must be approved by the local school board, the South Carolina Association of Independent Home Schools, or some other acceptable association. The teaching parent must possess a high school diploma or its equivalent. Standardized tests are required.

See Code of Laws of South Carolina Ann., 59-65-10, 40, 45, and 47.

South Dakota

Homeschools must provide instruction in the basic skills for a period of time equivalent to that spent in the public schools. Home education programs should include a core curriculum, as well as instruction in free enterprise, the U.S. and South Dakota constitutions, patriotism, and morals. Local school boards or officials may revoke homeschooling permission if families are not in compliance with established requirements. Standardized tests are required.

See South Dakota Comp. Law 13-27-2, 13-27-3, and 49-6-3001.

Tennessee

Parents must notify their local superintendents annually of their intent to homeschool. The teaching parent must have a high school diploma or GED to teach children in grades K–8, and a college degree to teach children in grades 7–12, unless the homeschool is affiliated with or under the supervision of a church school. Parents must maintain attendance records and homeschools must be in session for at least four hours per day, for the same number of days as the public schools. Standardized tests are required in grades 2, 5, 7, and 9; if the child tests six to nine months behind in core subjects, he or she may be required to enroll in school.

See Tennessee Code Ann. 49-6-3001 and 49-6-3050.

Texas

Homeschools in Texas are considered to be private schools. Parents do not need to notify the state or local school district of their intent to homeschool. Homeschoolers must use a written curriculum that covers the basic subjects of reading, spelling, grammar, math, and good citizenship. Standardized tests are not required.

See Texas Education Code 4.25 and 21.032 through 21.040.

Utah

Parents must submit an annual application form to their local school district for approval. Homeschools must teach the same courses required by the public schools: for grades K–6, language arts, math, science, social studies, arts, "healthy lifestyles," and information technologies. Standardized tests or some other method of evaluation are required.

See Utah Code Ann., 53A-11-1012.

Vermont

An annual "Enrollment Notice for Home Study Program" including a detailed curriculum description must be submitted for approval to the State Department of Education. Annual assessment is required by one of several different methods.

See Vermont Stat. Ann., Title 16, 1121, 16 (11), and 166b.

Virginia

Children may be taught at home by their parents, provided the primary instructor has a college degree or is a state certified teacher. Alternatively, homeschoolers may enroll in an approved correspondence course, participate in a program approved by their local superintendent, or produce a genuine religious objection to public schooling. Parents must submit an annual statement of intent and curriculum description to their local superintendents. Standardized tests are required; in the event that adequate educational progress is not demonstrated, "home instruction shall cease."

See Virginia Code 22.1-254.1.

Washington

Home-based instruction must include instruction in occupational education, science, math, language, social studies, history, health, reading, writing, spelling, and art and music appreciation. The primary instructor must have 45 college credits, must have completed a course in home instruction, must be supervised by a certified teacher, or must be deemed "qualified" by the local school board or designated school officials. Standardized tests or an assessment by "a certified person currently working in education" is required annually.

See Washington Rev. Code 28A.200.200 and 28A.225.10.

West Virginia

The home study program must be approved by the local school board or authorities; home teachers must possess a teacher's certificate, high school diploma, or at least four years' formal education above the pupil's. Standardized tests required.

See West Virginia Code 18-18-1.

Wisconsin

Homeschoolers must submit an annual statement of enrollment. Curricula not subject to approval. Standardized tests not required.

See Wisconsin Stat. Ann. 118.15 and 118.165.

Wyoming

Homeschool programs must be approved by the local school board or designated school officials. Each homeschool program must provide sequential instruction in reading, writing, math, civics, history, literature, and science. Parents must maintain attendance records. Standardized tests are not required.

See Wyoming Statute 21-4-101.

INDEPENDENT STUDY AND UMBRELLA SCHOOLS

Abbington Hill School
2140 Rte. 88, Suite 6-152
Bricktown, NJ 08742

(732) 892-4475
fax (732) 892-3737
e-mail: abbhill@aol.com
Web site:
www.abbingtonhillschool.com
　　Grades K–12

Cambridge Academy
3300 S.W. 34th Ave.
Suite 102
Ocala, FL 34474
(800) 252-3777
fax (904) 620-0492
Web site: www.home-school.com/
Mall/Cambridge/CambridgeAcad.
html
　　Grades 6–12

Christa McAuliffe Academy
3601 W. Washington Ave.
Yakima, WA 98903
(509) 575-4989
　　Grades K–12

Christian Liberty Academy
502 W. Euclid Ave.
Arlington Heights, IL 60004
(800) 348-0899
(708) 259-8736
Web site:
www.class.kingshighway.com
　　Grades K–12

Clonlara Home Based Education Program
1289 Jewett St.
Ann Arbor, MI 48104
(313) 769-4515
Web site: www.clonlara.org
　　Grades K–12

Home Study International
12501 Old Columbia Pike
Silver Spring, MD 20904
(301) 680-6570
(800) 782-4769
　　Preschool–College

Internet Home School
19475 Tomahawk Rd.
Apple Valley, CA 92307
(760) 242-0264
fax (760) 242-0284
e-mail:
fdm@internethomeschool.com
Web site:
www.internethomeschool.com
    Grades K–12

Kolbe Academy
1600 F Street
Napa, CA 94559
(707) 255-6499
fax (707) 255-1581
e-mail: kolbe@community.net
Web site: www.kolbe.org
    Grades K–12

Laurel Springs School
Box 1440
Ojai, CA 93024
(800) 377-5890
(805) 646-2473
fax (805) 646-0186
e-mail: info@laurelsprings.com
Web site: www.laurelsprings.com
    Grades K–12

**The Learning Community
International**
9085 Flamepool Way
Columbia, MD 21045
(410) 730-0073
    Grades K–12

Oak Meadow School
Box 740
Putney, VT 05346
(802) 387-2021
fax: (802) 387-5108
e-mail: oms@oakmeadow.com
Web site: www.oakmeadow.com
    Grades K–12

School of Tomorrow
Box 299000
Lewisville, TX 75029-9000
(972) 315-1776
Web site:
www.schooloftomorrow.com
    Grades K–12

Seton Home Study School
1350 Progress Dr.
Front Royal, VA 22630
(540) 636-9990
Web site: www.seton-home.org
    Grades K–12

Sycamore Tree
2179 Meyer Pl.
Costa Mesa, CA 92627
(714) 650-4466
Web site: www.sycamoretree.com
    Grades K–12

**Upattinas School and Resource
Center**
429 Greenridge Rd.
Glenmore, PA 19343
(610) 458-5138
Web site: chesco.com/upattinas
    Grades K–12

Westbridge Academy
1610 West Highland Ave.
Box 228
Chicago, IL 60660
(773) 743-3312
Web site:
www.flash.net/~wx3o/westbridge
    Grades K–12

Also see independent study/corre-
spondence high schools (page
168).

DOES HOMESCHOOLING WORK?

Examinations are formidable even to the best prepared,
for the greatest fool may ask more than the wisest man
can answer.

CHARLES CALEB COLTON

In an examination, those who do not wish to know ask
questions of those who cannot tell.

WALTER RALEIGH

Assessment in America starts at an early age. Preschool kids
are tested for "learning readiness" before admittance into
kindergarten; and a battery of tests, evaluations, examinations,
measurements, and comparisons dogs their steps through the
public school system. There's a scene in the movie *Baby Boom*,
in which Diane Keaton—a new adoptive mother—encounters
a trio of assessment-minded yuppie moms in the park. One of
the women is in tears because her toddler has failed the
preschool entrance exams. "If she doesn't get into the right

preschool," the mother sobs, "she's not going to get into the right kindergarten; if she doesn't get into the right kindergarten, I can forget about a good prep school and any *hope* of an Ivy League college." The daughter in question is two. It's funny—and then again, it isn't.

A 1997 Gallup poll indicated that 67 percent of the populace favors such modes of student assessment, coming down heavily in favor of standardized national tests to measure academic achievement. To date, such tests are routinely administered to students in almost all states (exceptions are Iowa and Nebraska). The standardized test is the most commonly accepted measure of whether or not the educational process is working. If you do well on the test, the assumption goes, you've been successfully educated; if not, you're intellectually hopeless. While standardized tests do not necessarily tell anyone much about an individual child's unique abilities or overall intelligence, they do seem to predict a child's chances of doing well in school—which, according to popular definition, is what education is all about anyway. Hence the relative importance of test scores to college admissions offices.

Hard on the heels of standardized national tests come demands for a standardized national curriculum—a set series of goals in English, mathematics, science, civics and government, history, geography, foreign languages, economics, and the arts—to be mastered by every child in America. Such a curriculum is a necessary corollary to a national test: if you're going to afflict students with a life-determining test, it's essential that they be taught the information to be covered. This drive to ensure universal competency, however, imposes a deadening uniformity on a process that cannot and should not be uniform. Children simply do not learn to order, and no worthwhile learning takes place in an atmosphere where the single most important question is "Will this be on the test?"

"All authorities get nervous when learning is conducted without a syllabus," write Postman and Weingartner (see page

10). "A syllabus not only prescribes what story lines you must follow (The War of 1812 in sixth grade, chromosomes in eleventh, South America in the ninth), it also prescribes the order in which your skills must be learned (spelling on Monday, grammar on Tuesday, vocabulary on Wednesday). This is called the 'sequential curriculum' and one has to visit the Ford Motor plant in Detroit in order to understand fully the assumptions on which it is based." Learning, however, as any true child-observer will tell you, is a messy and unpredictable process: it proceeds in fits and starts and mind-cramming binges, and it heads, lickety-split, down odd and unexpected pathways. And seldom do any two children head the same way at the same speed at the same time.

Try this: You're studying volcanoes. One child, fascinated by the ashy burial of Pompeii, will plunge into Roman history. "How long ago was Pompeii? Who dug it up? Do we have any pictures of it? How do ashes kill people?" Another, intrigued by geology, will sprint off in a different direction. "How hard is obsidian? Why do they call it volcanic *glass*? How hot is lava? What makes pumice float? Do different kinds of volcanoes make different kinds of igneous rocks?" And a third, utterly unenthusiastic about volcanoes, will drift off toward the living room to read *The Phantom Tollbooth*.

"Standardized tests measure nothing but test-taking skills," writes one homeschooler. "Tests are public prods to force kids to do what educators want," states Pat Farenga, homeschooling father of three, president of Holt Associates, the Cambridge-based national homeschooling organization. "Our children do not take standardized tests," writes a mother from Alabama. "We feel that the tests are too biased and put too much of an emotional burden on the test takers. Also our curriculum often stresses areas not covered on the tests." "We want our kids to think for themselves and make independent judgments," writes another homeschooling parent. "Tests encourage kids to go for good grades by parroting the most generally accepted beliefs."

"All children are subject to harm from standardized testing," writes another mother. "The younger the child, the more vulnerable he or she is to losing self-esteem, perhaps irreparably, in a testing situation."

Standardized tests come in all shapes and sizes, variously designed to assess everything from personality traits to general intelligence to one's ability to recall the multiplication tables, the rules of trigonometry, and salient points of the Treaty of Ghent. Those most commonly administered to schoolchildren can be roughly divided into two categories: aptitude tests, which assess intelligence, potential abilities, and/or general learning readiness; and achievement tests, which determine how well a kid has learned whatever he or she was supposed to be learning. Examples of the latter include the College Board's Scholastic Aptitude Test (SAT), which purports to identify those students who are most likely to perform well in college; and the Stanford-Binet IQ test, which attempts to quantify an individual's overall intelligence. The former—achievement tests—are generally given to public school students at two- to three-year intervals to assess educational progress. Examples include the California Achievement Tests (CAT), the Iowa Tests of Basic Skills (ITBS), and the Metropolitan Achievement Tests (MAT). Often states or local school districts demand that homeschoolers take achievement tests either annually or in the same years as the public school kids. In the public schools, classroom teachers are not held accountable for poor achievement test scores, and low scores are generally not seen—at least by school officials—as a good reason for pulling a child out of school. Homeschooling parents, unfortunately, *are* held accountable for low achievement test scores, which can be used as a reason to terminate homeschooling permission and insist that a child be enrolled in school.

◆ **April 16, 1990**

The state requires that kids take standardized tests in third grade, which—according to the form letter that we just received in the mail—means Josh. Since Josh has never so much as laid eyes on a test, we've acquired some practice booklets for the state-mandated California Achievement Tests (CAT), the examples in which—in my opinion—prove how moronic standardized tests are. The practice exercises are helpful, however, for learning how to take tests, which presumably is the point of the thing. Josh didn't know root words, prefixes, or suffixes—we'd never discussed these—but he caught on instantly once they were defined. He also had trouble with vowel sounds in words, which we're reviewing. Josh never did much in the way of phonics; once he learned to read, he found phonics totally boring.

◆ **April 17, 1990**

More test practice: vocabulary, root words, prefixes, suffixes, and more phonics. (Josh: Is this good for anything?) Test practice rapidly deteriorating. Josh hates it. He likes our homeschool projects much better—we're studying ancient Greece; also he's reading The Little Prince.

◆ **April 26, 1990**

Test practice with Josh. Synonyms, antonyms, picking appropriate word for sentences, and reading comprehension. Josh quite scornful of reading comprehension. There was also a section on fiction versus nonfiction: he was supposed to select, from a group of sentences, which one could or could not happen in the real world. Josh, who has a fertile imagination, fought this exercise tooth and nail. "How do they know that cats can't talk? Animals have their own languages. Look at dolphins." " 'The cats ran away' might not be real either. The sentence doesn't say how they ran away. Suppose they ran away in a car?" We will never get through this test.

I have my peeves too: I'm unimpressed with the test's vocabulary section, which runs toward urban slang: "sock" (meaning "hit"), "root" (meaning "cheer for a team"), and "sublet." These don't seem to me to be high-caliber general-interest vocabulary words.

◆ May 8, 1990

Persuaded Josh to try a bit more practice test, which was not easy. He tackled the spelling exercises and did beautifully, which fascinates me since he cannot spell. Apparently he has no trouble recognizing correctly spelled words, however, which is what the test tests for.

◆ May 14, 1990

Started CAT tests with Josh. He finished all the phonics and vocabulary sections.

◆ May 15, 1990

Josh: reading comprehension portion of CAT.

◆ May 16, 1990

Grammar and spelling portions of CAT.

◆ May 17, 1990

Josh finished the rest of the language sections on CAT. Word usage, ordering sentences in paragraphs, identifying parts of sentence (subject and predicate). Josh had never heard of subject and predicate, but I defined them rapidly and let him go for it.

◆ May 21, 1990

Addition and subtraction portions of CAT today. Josh struggled through it; he has a hard time with math. He knows how to perform the operations, but seems to make no concrete connections that help him understand the numbers. He can get an answer of 111 instead of 11 and be perfectly happy with it, sensible or no—and once he's done a problem, he is done. Checking, for

Josh, consists of looking vaguely at a problem and saying, "That's probably right."

◆ **May 22, 1990**

Multiplication and division sections of CAT. I simply loathe this test. We are wasting days on it. I am neglecting Ethan and Caleb while reviewing material/administering test to Josh—and once the test is over, Ethan and Caleb are raring to go, but Josh has had enough for the day. Even under these mild at-home conditions with as imperturbable a kid as Josh, this thing is stressful.

◆ **May 23, 1990**

Our homeschooling time continues to be swallowed by Josh's achievement test. Today: Mathematical Computations.

One aspect of this test that I find maddening is the totally alien and artificial atmosphere that they impose. No talking, no questions, no discussion, and an assigned time limit—nothing like we ever do in the normal course of homeschooling. Josh has questions, comments, and observations every two seconds—with me hissing anxiously, "Not now, Josh, this is a test!"—or he wants to get up in the middle of his timed fifteen minutes and make a cup of cocoa. Why is it useful to learn to take tests? This isn't doing anything positive for our homeschooling program, and if Josh were a less even tempered child, he'd be a wreck. Science and Social Studies sections still to go. I've peeked at them. They look asinine.

◆ **May 24, 1990**

Josh finished his achievement tests today. I am sending his answer booklet to the Bureau of Educational Measurements for official scoring, but I unofficially scored it using the "norms booklet" that came with the test. He did—I think—quite well, but I have my doubts about the scoring procedure. For example, in Test 6—Language Expression—Josh missed one (one!) out of thirty. According to my reading of the norms booklet, that puts him in the 79th percentile of third graders—so 20 percent of third-graders in the country got every single answer right? In Test 5—Language Mechanics—he missed 4 out of 35, which put him in the 51st percentile. (50 percent of the nation's third-graders do better than that?) Either the nation is much brighter than I had supposed or I am doing something wrong.

◆ June 7, 1990

Results of Josh's achievement tests arrived. His percentile scores: Word Analysis (42); Vocabulary (97); Reading Comprehension (90); Spelling (67); Language Mechanics (63); Language Expression (79); Mathematical Computation (66); Mathematical Applications (88); Science (93); and Social Studies (77).

The public school is very pleased with this (median total score for third-graders in our local public-school was 39.7) and the administrator who wrote us the congratulatory letter urges us to send Josh to school in September. Josh unimpressed. If these tests are the kind of thing they do in school, he says, he's never going.

And I find that I resent this entire scenario.

1. *Why on earth would we want to send Josh to a school whose test scores are well below the national average?*
2. *Why would we want to send Josh to a school whose idea of education is the ability to score well on this test?*
3. *Why are we, as homeschoolers, accountable to the public school system anyway?*

Most studies indicate that homeschooled students do well on standardized tests, scoring at or considerably above grade-level average. A 1996 study of 3,446 homeschooled kids, conducted by Brian Ray of the National Home Education Research Institute, showed average achievement test scores in the 87th percentile (the national average, by definition, is the 50th percentile). A 1992 survey of 10,750 homeschooled students sponsored by the Home School Legal Defense Asssociation similarly showed above-average test scores, ranging from the 56th to the 84th percentile, with a preponderance of test takers scoring somewhere in the 70s. In Kentucky in 1998, the 112 home-schooled students who took the SAT scored 20 to 22 percentile points above their public school peers in reading, language arts, and math. Fifth-, seventh-, and tenth-grade homeschoolers taking standardized tests in Arkansas earned composite scores in the 60th percentile, 12 to 14 percentile points higher than students in the public schools. The public schools are generally willing to accept grade-appropriate scores on standardized tests as evidence of acquired education; and it's easy to view success-ful test scores as proof of the academic pudding. Homeschool-ing, such test scores show, has justified itself by beating—or at least equaling—the public school system at its own game.

But the potential for better test scores, many homeschool-ing practitioners emphasize, is no reason in and of itself to homeschool. Homeschooling is a fruitful education option because it is *not* school, and test-driven demands to imitate the public school system's curriculum—"Does your child know the proper format for a friendly letter? The capital of North Dakota? The 17th president of the United States?"—inhibit alternative and independent learning styles. Education should not be equated with the ability to play Trivial Pursuit.

A greater issue here is that of *process* versus *product:* that is, is the way in which you learn as important as the outcome? Josh's test scores, for example, showed that his grasp of phonics was below average; his ability to read and understand what he had read, however, was superb. So what was the point here? Perhaps the phonics method—a process—didn't suit his learn-ing style. Perhaps he mastered reading by some eccentric method all his own. There are many paths to any educational Rome, and many of them are downright peculiar. Children often learn in unexpected ways, and mandated insistence upon a specific process—do it my way or not at all—can only defeat the purpose.

An increasingly accepted alternative to standardized testing as a means of measuring kids' progress is "portfolio assessment," which attempts to judge product—what a kid actually did—rather than the process by which he or she got there. A child's portfolio is a collection of his or her best work, testifying to a year's worth of amassed learning. Possible portfolio candidates are sample essays, short stories, and reports, reading lists, samples of artwork, photographs of science projects, and video- or audiotapes of kids in action. For formal assessment purposes, each portfolio entry should be dated and described. A professional educator will then evaluate the whole, assigning each item a score and ranking the child's overall performance. The schools have established restrictive criteria for grading portfolios, which gives me an irrepressible mental picture of an assessor painstakingly scoring Ethan's papier-mâché chicken on a scale of one to ten. Portfolio grading for just this reason—how *do* you evaluate a papier-mâché chicken?—has its problems; professional assessors often fail to agree, and scores thus may vary wildly. (A study of Vermont portfolio assessments found that scores assigned by different teachers agreed less than 50 percent of the time.) Still, such a system clearly gives an outsider a better grasp of a child's skills and abilities than a single standardized test score; and assembling a portfolio at least has potential for involving and interesting the child.

Creating Portfolios for Success in School, Work, and Life.
Kimeldorf, Martin; Free Spirit Publishing, 1994.
  How-tos and worksheets for assembling representative portfolios for persons of all ages.

Convincing the authorities that education is proceeding successfully, however, can be considerably less difficult than convincing yourself. How do you cope with those niggling three-o'clock-in-the-morning doubts? How do you, the concerned parent, know that learning is actually taking place? "How did you know," retorts one homeschooler, "when your kid learned how to ride a bicycle?" Most homeschoolers, when asked, produce story after story that illustrate active learning. The best and most accurate account of a child's learning process is found in such personal descriptions—which is why, for purposes of our homeschool program, we've always maintained detailed journals. A journal, to my mind, is the ideal form of record-keeping. Ours is a comprehensive account of our homeschooling life: a conglomeration of what we did, what the kids did, questions, responses, goals, hopes, worries, successes, failures, problems, and solutions. A homeschool journal, taken in its entirety, is an impressive and reassuring document. Like physical growth—which takes place in such tiny increments that we all have trouble coming to grips with the teenage six-footer who not all that long ago was the baby we toted around on one hip—learning is gradual. Immersion in daily homeschooling, with its ups and downs, steps forward and steps back, can mask the greater picture. Learning may be imperceptible in close-up but is unmistakable in the longer range.

"Face it," writes one homeschooler, "Johnny won't always be running around the house piecing together a solar collector out of old socks and bits of aluminum." "I never seem to have any of these stories," mourns another, "about how we use calculus to bake the breakfast muffins, how my nine-year-old reads *War and Peace* for fun, or how an interest in butterflies led to an apprenticeship with National Geographic and a trip to Bolivia." Maintain a journal, however, and it quickly becomes clear that over the past twelve months Johnny has done amazing numbers of things. An ongoing record allows you to see the blooming forest, rather than the trees.

The drawback to journal keeping is the time involved, which—especially if one is a chatty and thorough journal keeper—can be substantial. Alternatives to a diary-style journal include:

1. **Lists.** Jot down a quick list of what you and your kids have done over the course of each day. Date it.

2. **Photograph album or scrapbook.** Take photographs of ongoing projects, activities, and experiments; save souvenirs, maps, and fliers from field trips and extracurricular workshops. These, with a spot of notation here and there—"March 5: My Model Robot"—are a wonderful chronological (and visual) record of homeschooling experiences. One of ours, from 1994, includes photos of kids building geodesic domes, using a home-made "wind tunnel" to test a collection of paper airplanes, setting up a dialysis experiment on the kitchen counter, sprawled on the living-room floor with their italic handwriting workbooks, assembling a model DNA double helix, playing chess.

3. **Involving the children.** Convince the kids to help with the homeschool records in personal logs or a collaborative family journal. Encourage them to write down their daily activities. Keep personal (dated) book lists.

So does homeschooling work? That all depends on your definition of success. What do you want for your children? What do they want for themselves? Homeschooling is a versatile process, capable of expanding to reach and fulfill almost any goal or objective. By my lights, it works just fine.

What is success?
To laugh often and much;
To win the respect of intelligent people and the affection of children;
To earn the appreciation of honest critics and endure the betrayal of false friends;
To appreciate beauty;
To find the best in others;
To leave the world a bit better, whether by a healthy child, a garden patch or a redeemed social condition;
To know even one life has breathed easier because you have lived;
That is to have succeeded.

RALPH WALDO EMERSON
"WHAT IS SUCCESS?"

RESOURCES

INFORMATION PROVIDERS

ERIC Clearinghouse on Assessment and Evaluation
Catholic University of America
Education Department
Room 210, O'Boyle Hall
Washington, DC 20064
(202) 319-5120
Statistics, information, and evaluations of the all-important SAT.

National Center for Fair and Open Testing (FairTest)
342 Broadway
Cambridge, MA 02139
(617) 864-4810
fax (617) 497-2224
e-mail: FairTest@aol.com
Web site: www.fairtest.org
Should you take a test at all? This organization is concerned with a range of testing issues, among them the limitations of tests, test bias, and effective alternatives to tests. For a concise summary, see *Standardized Tests and Our Children: A Guide to Testing Reform* (FairTest, 1990). The organization also publishes a quarterly newsletter, *FairTest Examiner*.

BOOKS

Dr. Gary Gruber's Essential Guide to Test-Taking for Kids.
Gruber, Gary R.; William Morrow, 1986.
If you must take tests, you might as well be prepared. Helpful hints and how-tos for about-to-be-tested kids.

The Mismeasure of Man.
Gould, Stephen Jay; W. W. Norton, 1986.
A fascinating and scientific history of the uses and abuses of intelligence testing.

None of the Above: Behind the Myth of Scholastic Aptitude.
Owen, David; Houghton Mifflin, 1985.
A hard and analytical look at the SAT.

Princeton Review: Cracking the SAT and PSAT.
Robinson, Adam, and John Katzman; Villard Books, 1995.
Hints, how-tos, and sample tests, with an accompanying computer disk.

The Princeton Review series includes a large number of volumes on taking various kinds of standardized tests. See their Web site: www.review.com

Punished by Rewards: The Trouble With Gold Stars, Incentive Plans, A's, Praise, and Other Bribes.
Kohn, Alfie; Houghton Mifflin, 1995.
An attack on the idea that competition is beneficial and that school-generated rewards effectively promote learning.

Test Ready Series
Practice booklets for achievement
tests in all academic fields for kids
in grades 1–12.
Curriculum Associates, Inc.
5 Esquire Rd.
Box 2001
North Billerica, MA 01862-0901
(800) 225-0248
fax (508) 667-5706
e-mail: cainfo@curricassoc.com
Web site:
www.curricassoc.com/cainfo/

TEST SOURCES

Bayside School Services
Box 250
Kill Devil Hills, NC 27948
(800) 723-3057
e-mail: testing@freeyellow.com

Bob Jones University
1700 Wade Hampton Blvd.
Greenville, SC 29614
(800) 845-5731
(864) 242-5100
Web site: www.bju.edu

Family Learning Organization
Box 7250
Spokane, WA 99207-0247
(509) 467-2552

Christian Liberty Academy
502 W. Euclid Ave.
Arlington Heights, IL 60004
(800) 348-0899
(708) 259-8736
Web site:
www.class.kingshighway.com

The Sycamore Tree
2179 Meyer Place
Costa Mesa, CA 92627
(714) 650-4466
Web site: www.sycamoretree.com

THE _S_ QUESTION: WHAT ABOUT SOCIALIZATION? WILL MY KID GO TO THE PROM?

Friendship with oneself is all-important, because without
it one cannot be friends with anyone else in the world.

ELEANOR ROOSEVELT

When Caleb, our third son, was younger, he was fond of the
Berenstain Bear books by author/artists Jan and Stan
Berenstain, a near-endless series of short picture books about
the adventures of bumbling Papa Bear, moralizing Mama Bear,
and their offspring, Brother and Sister Bear. Brother and Sister
learn, in the course of various volumes, responsible money
management, healthful eating habits, the importance of manners and good sportsmanship, the evils of lying and selfishness,
and the best way to cope with peer pressure. All this, if not pre-

cisely great literature, was inoffensive enough, until we discovered the lesson that the Berenstains had to teach about socialization. In *The Berenstain Bears and the Nerdy Nephew*, Brother and Sister encounter Ferdy, an obnoxious young bear who makes their lives miserable. This is not all Ferdy's fault, however. Ferdy, explains Mama Bear, has been homeschooled by his parents and thus has never learned to get along with other cubs. Luckily a few days in school soon solve the problem, turning him into a nicer, more cooperative, and less nerdy bear.

The risk of inadequate socialization is a—if not *the*—prime objection to homeschooling, repeatedly voiced by professional educators and public school officials. Perhaps the most commonly asked question about homeschooling—so common that many practicing homeschoolers refer to it as "the S question"—is "What about socialization?" *Socialization*, defined, is a slippery catchall term, generally referring to the battery of "people skills" that allow people to cooperate in groups, form rewarding interpersonal relationships, and communicate effectively with each other. Boiled down to its simplest terms, socialization figures heavily in the list of life necessities compiled by Robert Fulghum in *All I Really Need to Know I Learned in Kindergarten*, to wit:

> *Share everything.*
> *Play fair.*
> *Don't hit people.*
> *Put things back where you found them.*
> *Clean up your own mess.*
> *Don't take things that aren't yours.*
> *Say you're sorry when you hurt somebody.*

There are a few more items on Mr. Fulghum's list, variously dealing with cleanliness, table manners, and appreciation of the world around us, but the above—the first seven—are his essential people skills. (Our family tacked on a few more caveats, variously banning screaming, interrupting, name-calling, and—in excited moments—the use of cereal spoons as weapons.) But are such social skills really learned in kindergarten? Do the schools transform ill-mannered elementary-aged hooligans into polite, poised, compassionate, and diplomatic adolescents? Are the schools really turning out kinder, gentler Americans?

Have you dropped in on any school playgrounds lately?

Children become socialized by observing the behaviors of the people around them and by interacting, in meaningful ways, with concerned and caring adults. Desirable social skills are not acquired en masse in the peculiarly structured social milieu of the public schools. A classroom of twenty-five seven-year-olds is not a real-world social situation; it's *school,* with its own unique sets of rules and regulations, many of which are aimed simply at keeping the kids quiet and sitting down. The inability of the schools to properly socialize their students is not the fault of the teachers or the kids involved. The structure of the system itself imposes limitations. Teachers simply don't have time to deal with the complexities of socialization; they're too busy exercising crowd control.

"Socialization is not a problem in homeschooling," writes a mother of two from Tennessee. "On the contrary, it's a problem in large group/school environments. Children don't naturally take to being herded together into large groups of peers. Even our Girl Scout troop would do better if it only had 7 or 8 girls. Homeschooling is a definite social advantage." "Our children are better socially adjusted *because* they do not attend school," writes a homeschooler from Minnesota. "They have time to participate in real life, real social activities. Sitting in a classroom with 20 to 30 other kids of the same age—all quietly at their desks, everything strictly organized—is not my idea of a good or natural social environment. Our kids relate to and socialize extremely well with people of all ages, from babies to the elderly. And we hear comments of praise concerning this all the time. Funny though—many don't make the connection between our children's social maturity and their freedom from school."

"The socialization 'problem' is a problem only in the minds of educators and other child 'welfare' specialists," states a home-schooling couple from northern New York. "What children need first is to establish a firmly-grounded sense of identity with their family unit. Secondarily, they need the opportunity that homeschoolers get to relate to people of all ages. Being sequestered for the majority of their waking hours with their biological 'identical twins' is counter-productive to producing useful citizens." "A healthy social life," writes Grace Llewellyn in *The Teenage Liberation Handbook,* "requires much more than indifferent daily acquaintanceship with 300 people born the same year you were."

While critics insist that the peer socialization experiences in school prepare a child for the hurly-burly of the real world—"Kids need the experience of having their blocks knocked down," states a homeschooling opponent from Texas—most homeschoolers counter that it's just such social negatives that they hope to avoid by keeping their children at home. "The social life of school," writes advocate John Holt uncompromisingly, "is generally snobbish, conformist, mean-spirited, fickle, ruthless, cruel, often violent, obsessed with competitive consumption, sex, and the use of harmful and often dangerous drugs." Is this the enriching social environment we want our children to know and accept as the "real world"?

Then there's the question of teamwork. "Cooperative learning situations," in which children are challenged to complete projects and solve problems as interactive groups, are a recent fad in public school classrooms. Such group endeavors, education experts explain, eliminate such undesirable traits as competitiveness and elitism while allowing participants to develop their social skills. Group problem-solving, unfortunately, has not worked out as planned: observers find that in such "cooperative" situations the brighter students often do a disproportionate share of the work, the slower students lose the impetus to do anything at all, and the independently creative get generally frustrated. While the ability to get along with others is unquestionably useful, the value of continual compromise or of routinely subordinating individual intellect to the demands of the group is at best doubtful. Our sons share and cooperate, but they also lean toward contrariness, independence, and individualism. Teams are fine in their place, but—as any corporate executive will tell you—no real problem was ever solved by a committee. Social conformity is highly overrated. Henry David Thoreau—by himself—chose to go to jail rather than pay taxes to support the Mexican War. Rosa Parks—stubbornly solo—refused to give up her seat on the Montgomery bus.

Thinking is like loving and dying—each of us must do it for himself.

JOSIAH ROYCE

While socialization—as in the ability to interact effectively with others—is clearly not a problem for homeschooled children, what about isolation? In John Goodlad's "Study of Schooling," a survey of 1,000 public school classrooms conducted in 1984, kids were asked what they liked best about school. The vast majority promptly answered "my friends." (Second-best response was "sports." Only 7 percent of kids mentioned "classes," and a mere 3 percent, "teachers.") The public schools do provide their students with a raft of ready-made acquaintances, if not bosom friends, and a battery of social activities—notably team sports—that homeschools in and of themselves cannot offer. This lack, as most homeschoolers loudly point out, does not mean that their children are isolated. The very word *homeschooling,* scoffs Pat Montgomery, founder of Michigan's innovative Clonlara School, seems to conjure up a "vision that kids are going to be locked in a room and toast is going to be slipped under the door." Instead, homeschooling parents, all too aware of the need for social enrichment, usually take care to provide their kids with creative alternatives to the school social scene. Homeschooled children participate in 4-H clubs, join scout troops, attend Sunday school, play on community sports teams. They take music, art, and dancing lessons, attend drama, woodworking, and pottery workshops, become involved in gymnastics, karate, and roller-skating. Many spend time each week in community service, variously volunteering at animal shelters, libraries, nursing homes, and day care centers.

A homeschool survey conducted by Suzanne MacDonald revealed that 62 percent of homeschooled kids participated in neighborhood activities; 57 percent in church groups and activities; 30 percent belonged to youth organizations; and 28 percent played on sports teams. A 1996 study of Christian homeschoolers by Brian Ray of the National Home Education Research Institute found similar evidence of enthusiastic social activity: of 5,402 surveyed kids, 87 percent participated in group play activities; 77 percent went to Sunday School; 48 percent played team sports; and 47 percent took music classes. Forty-two percent took various kinds of classes outside the home; 8 percent belonged to Boy or Girl Scout troops; 14 percent were 4-H members; 10 percent took dancing lessons; and 33 percent worked as community volunteers. All told, homeschooled kids on average spent ten hours a week with adults other than members of their immediate families, and eleven hours each week with nonsibling kids.

Many homeschoolers also participate in support groups—organizations of homeschooling families banded together for social activities, educational discussion, information and idea exchange, and—the support part—mutual encouragement and reassurance. Active support groups can have a lot to offer: group play sessions and field trips, parent-child exercise classes, joint projects and workshops, informational newsletters, and friends. Our support group experiences have included a children's singing class; group field trips to a cider mill, newspaper office, fire station, sheep farm, and hot-air balloon festival; weekly swimming sessions at a community pool; art workshops; and town cleanup projects. Other homeschoolers describe drama groups, kids' book discussion clubs, tree-planting projects, nature hikes, fossil-hunting expeditions, and woodworking workshops.

Support groups come in all flavors these days, small and large, local and state, tightly knit and loosely organized, Christian and secular, inclusive and exclusive. Since support groups are so varied, not every group will be congenial to every homeschooler. New homeschoolers should shop around. Attend a couple of meetings, introduce yourself, talk to people, ask questions. Do the support group members all subscribe to a single educational philosophy or do they represent an eclectic cross-section of ideas, theories, and opinions? *Exclusive* support groups have restricted memberships; some require new members to sign a statement of faith; others permit only bona fide church members to occupy leadership positions. *Inclusive* groups are open to all, but some groups are more cohesive in terms of philosophies and attitudes than others. How old are the children in the group? If they're all under seven, and you've got three teenagers, your kids may be happier elsewhere. What kinds of activities does the group participate in? How open is the group to new suggestions and ideas?

From my homeschool journal:

◆ **December 17, 1990**

I'm feeling more and more awkward in our present homeschool group. The people are—for the most part—very nice; and our kids enjoy playing with their kids, but all of them—except us—go to the same church, and the group is very Christian in its orientation. This past Saturday morning I went to a get-together for mothers, ostensibly to plan the next few months' worth of field trips. The meeting, however, was essentially a prayer meeting. It opened with a prayer and ended with a prayer; members took turns reading from the Bible (everyone brought their own Bible) and all joined in singing hymns. I'm not sure what to do. The boys have made some friends; and many of the group activities are fun; but we're clearly on the periphery of the group social scene because of our secular philosophy. One of the mothers invited all the homeschooled kids in the group to her son's birthday party—except our boys, which hurt their feelings. (Mine too.)

◆ **August 15, 1991**

A brainstorming session today with the parents in our local support group. The group is making arrangements for a series of Friday classes for homeschoolers to start this fall. The classes will be headed by the group's minister and his wife, who are home-schooling their four children—all group members except us attend the same church—and will be held at the church. Plans are in the works for art lessons, writing workshops, singing sessions, and Bible classes. I volunteered to teach a science class, but no one was interested—for which, to be honest, I can't blame them, given my negative take on creationism. I'm not sure what to do. These are (mostly) pleasant people, but they're also a very cohesive group—spiritually, academically, and philosophically—and we simply do not belong. This support group isn't supportive for me.

A letter from Terry, my homeschooling pen pal—mother of two—helped put my support group worries in perspective. Terry and I met at a children's gymnastics class, where two of my sons and one of hers were learning to tumble, jump on the trampoline, turn cartwheels, and stand on their heads. Terry and her husband, Ron, a pilot and colonel in the Marine Corps, were homeschooling their two boys, John and Jason. Our meeting was the start of a beautiful and multimembered friendship. Despite many moves—the Marines don't stay put—Terry and I have kept up a long and detailed homeschool correspondence. Our exchange of letters—equal parts agony column, therapy group, suggestion box, and just plain bolstering—has always been a lifeline through the inevitable ups and downs of the homeschool experience.

HOMESCHOOL PEN PALS

For adults and children seeking homeschooling pen pals, see the bimonthly listings in *Home Education Magazine* (page 28) or *Growing Without Schooling* (page 28), or try some of the many chat groups and discussion forums currently available on-line (page 30).

"Follow your instincts," Terry wrote from Arizona. "You don't feel that you and the boys belong, so don't belong. It hurts to mingle goodheartedly with people who don't approve of you, don't accept you, don't share your philosophy. If you are like me, you faithfully go to the meetings and sit quietly, not really feeling happy or fulfilled, while the boys play all over the playground, getting the exercise and socialization you feel they should have, and then on the way home in the car you sigh and mutter your complaints and frustrations aloud to the semi-attentive audience of children, who are hot, thirsty, and tired. They pick up on your mood and wonder why you are all home-schooling anyway, if it is no good."

◆ **November 18, 1991**

I've connected—through a chance meeting at the public library—with a secular homeschool group. Most of the kids are on the young end of the scale—three- to six-year-olds—but there are a few around Josh and Ethan's age. They all skate together every Friday afternoon, which prospect has the boys very excited; they also sponsor a book discussion group for the older children that meets twice a month. This month's selection is Arthur Ransome's Swallows and Amazons; *in anticipation, Josh is already halfway through it. It's a very mixed group of people, all using different materials and approaches to home education, which makes for a lot of interesting give and take. Plans are under way for pottery classes and science sessions at our house; one of the other mothers has volunteered to teach coeducational sewing.*

Many homeschoolers, repeatedly cautioned about the dangers of under-socialization, overreact, soon finding themselves overcommitted and in over their social heads. In our first years of homeschooling, we fell into just such social traps. We have always lived in isolated portions of the country, devoid of neighbors. Heroic measures, I decided, were needed to provide the boys with adequate group interactions. We ended up frenziedly on the road, traveling from class to group field trip to extracurricular activity to club to play group. Enough socialization can rapidly become too much.

A limited number of group activities has always worked better for us than a fast-track social round. As important as socialization is its opposite number: the ability to enjoy solitude, to make fruitful and satisfying use of time spent alone. "My son expressed this view of socialization last week," a homeschooling friend writes, "and I find myself agreeing with him. 'Let's just stay home, Mom, and read and do our own projects. All this running here and there to get educated makes me tired.' I am thinking seriously of becoming *less* social this year and certainly more selective about where and how we spend our precious time. I don't like spending a whole morning at some activity that we really don't enjoy, with a lot of judgmental mothers and ill-behaved children, just so my kids can have continual human companionship. I'd rather do less, with the two or three families whose company is truly rewarding."

Learning how to spend time alone, many homeschoolers argue, is just as important as learning how to interact in a group. Children accustomed to an intensive round of school hours and extracurricular activities often have difficulty dealing with empty time. And it's just this empty time that is so essential to intellectual growth: the time to think and assimilate, to daydream and imagine. "Learning to get along with oneself," writes one homeschooler, "is at least as crucial as forming childhood relationships." Some children, furthermore, simply learn better by themselves. Not all of us want or need the same amount of social interaction.

I think you should learn, of course, and some days you must learn a great deal. But you should also have days when you allow what is already in you to swell up inside of you until it touches everything. And you can feel it inside you. If you never take time out to let that happen, then you just accumulate facts, and they begin to rattle around inside of you. You can make noise with them, but never really feel anything with them. It's hollow.

E. L. KONIGSBERG
FROM THE MIXED-UP FILES OF MRS. BASIL E. FRANKWEILER

Any fool can be fussy and rid himself of energy all over the place, but a man has to have something in him before he can settle down to do nothing.

J. B. PRIESTLEY

Our kids, so far, seem to function reasonably well either alone or in a group, with persons of all ages, from the very young to the very old. They take violin and piano lessons, play in the local youth orchestra, and volunteer at the county humane society. They ski and skate with a local homeschool support group. One of them takes classes at the local community college. One of them is an extrovert, one of them is an introvert, and one of them alternates cheerfully between the two. None of them, so far, has gone—or expressed any desire to go—to a prom.

RESOURCES

Books

A Sense of Self: Listening to Homeschooled Adolescent Girls.
Sheffer, Susannah; Heinemann, 1995.
Recent research by Harvard psychologist Carol Gilligan and coworkers indicates that conventionally schooled adolescent girls suffer drastic drops in self-confidence, assertiveness, self-esteem, and—often—academic achievement. Sheffer shows one possible solution to this problem: educate your daughters at home. Homeschooled adolescent girls are notably more self-confident than their public school peers.

Support Group Guide
California Homeschool Network
Box 44
Vineburg, CA 95487-0044
A 44-page publication of the California Homeschool Network covering everything you ever wanted to know about homeschool support groups, including information on starting a group, suggestions for organization and operation, and how-tos for publishing a group newsletter. $8

Strengths of Their Own: Home Schoolers Across America.
Ray, Brian; NHERI Publications, 1997.
A detailed statistical survey of 1,657 Christian homeschool families, variously analyzing family characteristics and student levels of academic achievement and social activity.

Homeschool Support Groups

For a comprehensive state-by-state list of homeschool support groups, see the Appendix on page 175.

Growing Without Schooling
2380 Massachusetts Ave.
Suite 104
Cambridge, MA 02140-1226
(617) 864-3100
fax (617) 864-9235
e-mail: holtgws@erols.com
Web site: www.holtgws.com

Home Education Magazine
Box 1083
Tonasket, WA 98855-1083
(509) 486-1351
(800) 236-3278
fax (509) 486-2753
e-mail:
HEM@home-ed-magazine.com
Web site:
www.home-ed-magazine.com

Home School Organizations
Web site: www.home-school.com/Groups/OrgList.html

Homeschooling Resources
Web site: www.alumni.caltech.edu/~casner/statelist.html

Regional and Worldwide Homeschooling
Web site: homeschooling.miningco.com/library/regional/blRegion.htm

TO SCHOOL OR NOT TO SCHOOL: HOMESCHOOLING HOW-TOS

A magnificent education, as countless examples attest, can come from nothing more than reading and writing.

RICHARD MITCHELL
THE GRAVES OF ACADEME

I forget what I was taught. I only remember what I have learnt.

PATRICK WHITE

Knowing only what is necessary makes life dull and begins the regression of knowledge.

BENJAMIN FRANKLIN

Education is not the filling of a pail, but the lighting of a fire.

WILLIAM BUTLER YEATS

"But what do you *do* all day?" a friend with two children in private school once asked me. "*How* do you homeschool?"

Methods of homeschooling are as many and varied as the homeschoolers themselves. Techniques range from the highly structured to the casually loose. Some families establish traditional "schools at home," complete with school-style desks and textbooks, set hours, lesson plans, and an introductory Pledge of Allegiance to the American flag; others subscribe to the philosophy of "unschooling," rejecting formal curricula in favor of "natural" learning, evolving in the course of daily life as kids actively investigate and pursue their own interests. And many employ a creative mix of the two, alternating structured study with untrammeled child-directed learning. This last best describes our approach to home education. We generally use a structured approach to the basics—reading, writing, mathematics—paired with an open approach to the kids' many and multifaceted interests.

All of the above works. There is *no* "right way" to homeschool: kids, with their unique assortments of likes, dislikes, interests, ambitions, and learning styles, respond very differently to different modes of education. "My kids teach me how to teach," writes one homeschooler, and nothing could be more descriptive of home education. Parents who spend time with their children soon discover how best to help their children learn.

"When we first started homeschooling," writes a mother from West Virginia, "we used a very structured school-like curriculum because our kids all wanted report cards like the neighbors. After a few months of A's, however, they lost interest, and now we use an unstructured method, supplemented with public television." "We've tried it all!" write the parents of two from Indiana. "We've had contracts, daily schedules, very structured, loosely structured, outside tutors—and now we're in a 'free school' mode. The kids decide if, when, and what they want to study." "We read," writes a Virginia family. "Read, read, read. Two or more hours a day, plus a 'long' book read chapter by chapter every evening. Our whole life is learning. We live in the country. Nature lessons abound. Gardening, housework, cooking—all are full of lessons." "We tried a nonstructured approach," writes an Alabama homeschooler, "but the kids disliked it. Now we use a semi-strict structured approach—a correspondence course with daily instructions and assignments—and it works *very* well."

Too much rigidity on the part of teachers should be followed by a brisk spirit of insubordination on the part of the taught.

AGNES REPPLIER
WRITER AND HISTORIAN

Our boys, especially when younger, preferred a certain predictable rhythm to their days. Mathematics and writing, for example, were learned better when practiced daily, enabling the boys to see and appreciate the benefits of steady cumulative effort. Other subjects were covered in less structured fashion, following the dictum "Strike when the iron is hot." When a museum trip inspired a fascination with knights, armor, castles, tournaments, and all things medieval, we studied—it was an irresistible force—the Middle Ages. When a reading of *The Indian in the Cupboard* (Lynne Reid Banks) triggered an interest in Indian dwellings—"What did a longhouse *really* look like? How long was it?" "Did the same Indians build longhouses and tepees?" "What was a tepee made out of?" "How many people could fit in a tepee?" "Did the Indians build *furniture?*"—we read books about Indian habitats, built models of longhouses and tepees, and visited museum exhibits featuring Indian lifestyles and houses. Child-led learning of this sort generates an immense array of interests, queries, and curiosities. Our boys, seemingly without batting an eye, could leap from entomology to ancient China to modern architecture, eager to dissect grasshoppers, raise silkworms, experiment with Chinese brush painting, and build a model of the Eiffel Tower. This multiplicity of interests is mind-broadening, intellectually exciting, and just plain fun—and giving the boys the opportunity to pursue these was a dominant factor in our decision to homeschool.

◆ **May 8, 1991**

Caleb had a horrendous fall on his bicycle yesterday; landed face-first on a rock and smashed his front teeth. We careened off on an emergency trip to the dentist, where all the boys learned a great deal about X rays, lidocaine, tooth structure, dental tools, and the like, but this was not my preferred mode of education. Caleb, poor baby, had two teeth pulled. He put one in an envelope addressed to the tooth fairy and saved the other for dissection— perversely, this incident has aroused great interest in the study of teeth. Which is what we did today, though the very mention of teeth still makes me cringe.

The boys took turns looking through several picture books about sharks, after which we read—jointly—the Sharks *Zoobook, with special attention to shark teeth. The boys all drew shark pictures: Ethan and Caleb, very careful scientific drawings of sharks based on the diagrams in the Zoobook; Josh, a captioned shark cartoon. Discussed carnivores, herbivores, and omnivores, and the way teeth reflect specific food habits. Looked up pictures of elephant teeth in the* Elephants Zoobook. *Ethan: "Remember the mammoth tooth in the museum in Colorado? It looked like a giant clam!"*

The boys identified incisors, canines, bicuspids, and molars in their own mouths with the aid of a mirror; and Josh drew a clever little cartoon illustrating each tooth type. Discussed how different teeth are used in eating: "If you bite an apple, first you take a big slice with your incisors." "Incisors! That's what Caleb knocked out on the rock!" (Me: shudder.) "What teeth do you use when you chew a piece of steak?" "My filling was in a molar!"

Then we found a diagram of the inner structure of the tooth in The Human Body and How It Works (Giovanni Caselli), and defined the various parts of a tooth and their functions.

Kids: "Which is harder—bones or teeth?" "How does calcium get in your teeth?" "Does milk make teeth white?" "Are our teeth made of ivory, like an elephant's teeth are?" "Why does a dentist have to drill your teeth when you get a cavity?"

We discussed what causes cavities and toothaches, and the boys drew and labeled tooth diagrams. We examined Caleb's knocked-out tooth—he has it in a little blue plastic box, given to him by the dentist—and identified enamel, dentin, and root. Explained how the roots of baby teeth are resorbed by adult teeth, so when baby teeth fall out—as opposed to being knocked out— they are rootless. Caleb then smashed his tooth with a hammer to see what was inside—"This is where the nerves are!"

◆ May 9, 1991

More teeth. We read about colonial tooth-pulling practices and the boys—appalled—invented assorted painless tooth-extracting machines. Reviewed causes of cavities and defined anaesthetic. "Are there lots of different kinds of anesthetics?" "How are they different?" "What kind did Caleb have?"

Covered unusual teeth: read about elephants and their tusks in the Elephants Zoobook, drew elephant pictures, discussed ancestral elephants, and read If You Lived in the Days of the Wild Mammoth Hunters (Mary Elting and Franklin Folsom). Talked about ivory and ivory poachers.

Read Snakes Are Hunters (Patricia Lauber), concentrating on the structure and function of fangs; the boys all drew spectacular and highly imaginative poisonous snakes. "What's the most poisonous snake in the world?" "When a rattlesnake bites you, why doesn't it always kill you?"

Discussed crocodiles and their teeth, in enthusiastic detail.

Defined deciduous teeth and calculated how many more teeth adults have than kids.

"How big were dinosaur teeth? How long are rattlesnake teeth? If a dog bites you, why do you get rabies?"

Trip to the library after lunch, during which the boys made a beeline for books about sharks, crocodiles, and snakes.

On the other hand, an eclectic collection of topics without some connecting framework to hang them on runs a risk of becoming a fragmented and discombobulating learning experience. Child-led learning, in our hands, seemed to work best when balanced by continuity. New knowledge was best absorbed when logically connected to an ordered central core.

So what's an ordered central core? How to build an effective and coherent curriculum? Some homeschoolers design or purchase a packaged curriculum based on that of the public schools, which supposedly roughly parallels the intellectual development of the average child. For those parents designing their own course of study, many publications include detailed sequential lists of what children are expected to master in grades K–12. World Book Educational Products, for example, distributes a free booklet, *Typical Course of Study: Kindergarten Through Grade 12,* an abbreviated year-by-year list of the concepts students are expected to cover in the fields of language arts, math, science, social studies, and health and safety. A more detailed summary of the same material in book form can be found in The Core Knowledge Series by E. D. Hirsch Jr.: the series includes one book for each of the first seven grades (K–6), each describing the required fundamentals for each age group in the fields of math, science, history, geography, language arts, technology, and the arts, with illustrations, photographs, maps, and the texts of recommended stories and book excerpts. In some states, specific homeschool regulations spell out required material to be covered at each grade level.

Typical Course of Study: Kindergarten Through Grade 12.
Free from World Book Educational Products, Box 980, Orland Park,
IL 60462; (708) 873-1533.

*The Core Knowledge Series: What Your Kindergartener (First-Grader,
etc.) Needs to Know: Preparing Your Child for a Lifetime of Learning.*
Hirsch, E. D. Jr.; Doubleday.

Packaged curricula, which include all grade-appropriate workbooks, texts, and lesson plans, are often the method of choice for those homeschoolers who prefer a structured "school at home." Others prefer to invent their own curricula, thus designing programs of study that are more in tune with their children's personalities, interests, learning styles, and needs. We've always made it a habit to sit down together one afternoon in August and discuss plans for the upcoming nonschool year. The boys list topics they'd most like to study; Randy and I make a few suggestions—putting in our two cents in support of the basics; and the end result is an annual study plan. My homeschool journals record lists of plans to learn about papermaking, rabbits, knights and castles, spaceships, lasers, whales, and life in ancient Egypt. Caleb, our youngest son, the summer he was four, had only two educational goals: to tame a squirrel and to ride the bumper cars at the county fair. The summer he was twelve, ambitions had expanded: he wanted to study astronomy and Latin, take a class in glassblowing, go on an archaeological dig, and learn to play the oboe. Ethan, last summer, planned to study computer programming, electronics, and nanotechnology—"*Nanotechnology?*" I squeaked nervously—and Josh announced his intentions to write a novel, read, study entomology and cell biology, and continue piano lessons. Not all of these aspirations are always fulfilled—we never did track down a formal class in glassblowing—but we do our best, fleshing out each child's program as needed. (Caleb: literature; Ethan: writing skills; Josh: geometry.)

What are my plans for the fall? I'm doing a unit study on the habits of striped bass and shore birds. My lab instruments are fishing rods and binoculars.

EARL GARY STEVENS, HOMESCHOOLER IN MAINE

Until the boys reached high school age, their learning styles seemed to mesh best with what are popularly called "unit studies": assorted projects, activities, and reading materials covering a range of academic disciplines, all centered around a single unifying theme. Our unit studies typically featured a home-written information-and-activity book—topics have included the Civil War, frogs, stars, trees, eyes, bees, Vikings, eclipses, statistics, and mapmaking—along with related craft and science kits, and fiction and nonfiction books, plus much discussion, conversation, and answering of questions. Many of our unit studies, in turn, were generated from the calendar, variously highlighting the birthdays of famous persons, historical anniversaries, and miscellaneous unusual holidays. For example, we've celebrated (in eccentric detail) the birthdays of George Washington Carver, Benjamin Franklin, Louis Braille, Amelia Earhart, Thomas Jefferson, Tycho Brahe, Susan B. Anthony, Helen Keller, and P. T. Barnum; and commemorated the launching of Sputnik, the Wright brothers' flight at Kitty Hawk, the opening of the Erie Canal, the completion of the transcontinental railroad, the opening of Tutankhamen's tomb, and the discovery of gold at Sutter's Mill.

And many topics simply popped up serendipitously—witness Caleb's teeth—depending on the boys' interests at the time. An afternoon class at a local museum, for example, plunged them into a study of Navajo Indians; a visit to a falconer led to an interest in raptors. Other homeschoolers describe similar forays into thematic learning. A New York City mother tells of her son's study of ancient Rome: he prowled the Roman history section of the Metropolitan Museum of Art, watched the movies *Spartacus* and *Ben-Hur,* read *I, Claudius,* studied Latin, and experimented with Roman cooking. A Virginia family used their eighteenth-century farmhouse as a jumping-off point for studying regional history, family genealogy, colonial architecture and everyday life, and the multi-headed craft of building restoration. One of my favorite homeschooling stories is that of one New York family's experience in learning how to make maple syrup. They began by visiting local syrup makers to learn about the process and study their equipment, and by going to the library to track down relevant books (for persons of all ages). They identified and tapped maple trees, and collected sap, calculating along the way how much sap they collected per tree and how much syrup this would produce when boiled down. They collaborated on building an evaporator. They boiled their sap, learning about temperature, viscosity, and sugar concentration. They toured a large-scale sugarhouse. And finally they threw a celebratory pancake-and-syrup breakfast party and whipped up a batch of maple sugar candy. All in all, the project encompassed history, botany, physics, chemistry, and home economics—to say nothing of teamwork, socialization, and joint learning. This rich and integrated form of learning is what one parent calls "life-school"—meaning that the children's education takes place naturally in the course of daily living.

One invaluable aspect of "life-school"—and perhaps the one most essential element of our homeschooling—is simply relaxed time to talk. Our children's education has developed from a base of conversation, question, and answer—their questions, that is, not ours. A questioning kid inevitably is an interested and motivated kid. "I continually try to surprise my kids with interesting facts and new ideas," writes one homeschooling parent, "and if they ask questions, I go with it." A question

First-hand knowledge is the ultimate basis of intellectual life. To a large extent book-learning conveys second-hand information, and as such can never rise to the importance of immediate practice.

ALFRED NORTH WHITEHEAD

Experiential learning is the kind that sticks.

HOMESCHOOLING MOTHER, VERMONT

is a desire to know—and without that desire, learning doesn't happen. "How big is the sun?" "What do grasshoppers eat?" "What's inside a battery?" "How does the television work?" "What makes a rainbow?" John Goodlad's landmark "Study of Schooling" revealed that 96 percent of the questions asked in public school classrooms are directed by teachers at students and, of these, most are one-answer mini-quizzes aimed at discovering whether or not Johnny did his homework. This approach, write Postman and Weingartner, sends the message "that recall—particularly the recall of random facts—is the highest form of intellectual achievement." The real questions—the substantive, thought-provoking questions—are those to which there are many answers, conflicting answers, or even no answers at all. Chewing these over takes time. "How could Thomas Jefferson write the Declaration of Independence and then never free his slaves?" "Why are there so many wars over religion?" "Are computers better than books?" "Should you be able to do anything you want with your own land? If you own a forest, should you be allowed to cut down all the trees?" "How come some people are so rich and some are so poor?"

Not all questions and not all hands-on experiences are equally valuable, however, which is where—in the course of our homeschooling program—a touch of parental guidance comes in. Sometimes such guidance merely consists of providing a curiosity-provoking learning environment. Tinker with the microscope, drag out the treadle sewing machine, or experiment with watercolor paints, and the kids will join in; produce a building set or a science kit, and the kids will tackle it. "Want your kids to read a particular book?" one homeschooler asks. "Just throw it on the couch!" For some subjects, we use—or have used—a more structured approach to learning. These, for the most part, are what writer Clifton Fadiman calls "generative subjects": those essential subjects that give students the power to learn all else for themselves, notably reading, writing, and mathematics. Mastering these disciplines generally requires sequence, practice, and effort—which, in and of itself, teaches a lesson that is useful for children to learn. Some things are difficult, but the payoff is infinitely rewarding, granting as it does—Clifton Fadiman again—"the magnificent pleasure of stretching the mind."

What do homeschoolers do all year?

Here are a pair of sample curricula, prepared for and approved by the public school system:

Homeschool Curriculum 1990–1991

Joshua S. Rupp (approximately 4th grade)
Ethan S. Rupp (approximately 1st/2d grade)
Caleb B. Rupp (approximately kindergarten)

Our curriculum consists primarily of varied history- and science-centered topics, providing opportunities for "child-directed integrated learning"—plus a daily dose of the basics in reading, writing, and arithmetic. A major resource used for the former purpose is a series of home-written interactive workbooks (samples enclosed). We usually complete one of these topic-centered books in one to three weeks (depending on the children's interest and the complexity of the topic), using them as starting points for additional reading, research, and/or hands-on projects.

This is thus the general pattern for our homeschool program: we start out with a preselected central topic and branch out in a number of different directions, depending on the children's responses and interests. This past spring, for example, we spent some weeks studying ancient Greece. We read a large number of books on ancient Greek lifestyles and a lot of Greek mythology, made a mural of the Greek gods and goddesses, built clay models of the Parthenon, crushed grapes and made wine (which included studying yeast under the microscope, defining fermentation, reading about the chemistry of wine making, setting up a wine-making experiment with proper controls, and tasting small awful sips of the finished products), reconstructed a Greek black-figure vase using a commercial archaeology kit, visited a local art museum to tour the Greek/Roman collection, learned to write our names using the Greek alphabet, listened to a rendition of the *Odyssey* on cassette tapes, read about Archimedes and demonstrated his famous Principle, learned the difference between the diameter and the circumference of a circle, and the mathematical use of pi, located Greece and associated countries on the world map, and so on.

Ongoing projects include calendar making at the beginning of each month, maintaining a daily temperature graph, recording the phases of the moon, journal writing, publishing a monthly family newsletter, celebrating the birthdays of famous people (with associated projects and reading), celebrating the anniversaries of states' admission to the Union (ditto), and making a history timeline.

READING

Joshua (nine) is a voracious and enthusiastic reader. Basically he chooses his own reading material, from weekly trips to the public library, from the home bookcases (we have a *lot* of books), and from children's book catalogs, of which we get many. This works, so we leave him alone and let nature take its course. Last year he whipped through an impressive number of books, including the short stories of Edgar Allan Poe, T. S. Eliot's *Old Possum's Book of Practical Cats,* the poems of Ogden Nash, Mordecai Richler's *Jacob Two-Two* books, Roald Dahl's *Matilda, The Witches, The BFG,* and *James and the Giant Peach,* Beverly Cleary's *The Mouse on the Motorcycle* series, the entire *Tin Tin* series by Hergé, and a great deal of Greek mythology. We often suggest a "book of the week" for Josh, selecting something a little more challenging or unusual than he might come up with on his own. This year we're also planning to run through the books on the fourth-grade-level Junior Great Books reading list. The Great Books program is designed to promote "critical silent reading" by participating kids, to be accompanied by group discussions on various philosophically fuzzy aspects of the stories. ("*Why* did the giant's wife hide Jack?" "*Why* did the knight get eaten by the fifty-first dragon?") We think we could all have fun with this on a small scale at home. We plan to encourage Josh to keep a book journal or diary. (However, we tried this last year too. It fizzled.)

Ethan (seven) can read, in a painful Pat the Fat Cat fashion, sounding each word out as he goes. He doesn't generally read to himself; however, he loves to be read *to* and will spend considerable time looking through books, which I take as a positive sign. Last year we did a lot of phonetic exercises using the SRA DISTAR reading program (*Teach Your Child to Read in 100 Easy Lessons;* Engelmann, Haddox, and Bruner), which I suspect was a mistake. Ethan was initally enthusiastic—he's a very mechanically minded child, and I think saw phonics as a logical means of cracking the reading puzzle—but gradually became bored and disenchanted with the whole process. We continued to struggle along through the year, with Ethan becoming increasingly resistant and upset. He did master phonics, which was useful on one front (see Writing, below), but still hasn't made the necessary transition from phonics to comfortable whole-word recognition. This year we're dropping formal phonics-type reading programs: my assessment is that they're dull, off-putting, and no way to learn to read. Instead, we're simply going to keep reading together daily, books he likes, by the bale. We will also continue phonics using our own homemade workbooks, which (1) he enjoys, and which (2) approach phonics from a number of different angles. Under *B,* for example, the kids will make boats, butter, and bread, string beads, read Sylvia Plath's *The Bed Book* and design their own magical beds, plus practice reading, writing, and inventing stories with selected *B* words.

Caleb (five) also used the DISTAR program last year, working through the first thirty lessons or so. (He wasn't enthralled with it, but liked the idea of doing the same thing Ethan was doing, which is always seductive to the youngest child.) Caleb reads at about the same level as Ethan, but differently—he's a whole-word recognizer, and is thus much more comfortable with reading (or trying to). He's also a dedicated book looker, and seems to be well on his way to putting it all together on his own. We will read together daily. He will also participate in our home-designed phonics program along with Ethan.

I read with all the boys for at least two hours a day, usually at lunchtime and in the evening before bed. We generally have one long chapter book going, plus assorted shorter books.

Reading resources: Library cards, a personal library of over 1,000 children's books, both fiction and nonfiction, numerous magazine subscriptions, three of them specifically targeted toward children (*Cricket, Faces,* and *Ranger Rick*), "Reading and Me" and "Reader Rabbit" phonics and word recognition computer programs, "Sing, Spell, Read, and Write" and DISTAR phonics/reading programs, multiple dictionaries and reference works, including the *Oxford English Dictionary,* a slightly outdated *Encyclopaedia Britannica, Bartlett's Familiar Quotations, Roget's Thesaurus,* and two bookwormish parents.

WRITING

Joshua, whose motor coordination is such that he falls over his own feet while walking across the room, has slovenly but readable handwriting. He mastered cursive handwriting this past year, but generally still prints if given his choice. He writes constantly—stories, poems, comic strips, letters to a pen pal in California, a sporadic diary—but he has many more ideas than he manages to get down on paper. He finds the physical act of writing difficult and restrictive, which frustrates him.

Ethan, whose motor coordination is excellent, prints neatly (though is shaky in his knowledge of lowercase letters) and is eager to learn cursive handwriting. To this end, he has just adopted a couple of commercial handwriting books and is busily working through them. He has also recently begun writing simple stories of his own, using his newly acquired knowledge of phonics (see Reading, above) to invent spellings.

Caleb prints, in capitals. He's at the CALEB, MOM, DAD, and I LOVE YOU stage.

We're aiming for daily creative writing this year. Josh already keeps a diary (when the fit takes him); the present plan is for everyone to start writing/illustrating a daily journal. (We'll see how this goes.) We also plan to continue publishing our monthly newsletter, which includes family news, stories, poems, jokes, riddles, and artwork by the kids. Copies are sent to friends and relatives. We plan to continue our group poetry-writing sessions, in part based on projects proposed in Kenneth Koch's *Rose, Where Did You Get That Red?* The boys all like poetry.

We have recently acquired a children's typing program for our computer and plan to encourage all three boys to type and make more extensive use of the word processor. I think this will be particularly helpful to Josh, whose brain routinely outruns his hand power. (To date, Josh has not shown much computer interest.) We also plan to experiment with calligraphy, which I believe may lure the boys into handwriting practice via artistic novelty.

Writing resources: Several books of children's writing projects, among them *The Creative Journal for Children* (Capacchione), *Families Writing* (Stillman), *Rose, Where Did You Get That Red?*, and *Wishes, Lies, and Dreams* (Koch), and *Beyond Words: Writing Poetry With Children* (McKim and Steinbergh); a computer with word processor capacity; and lots of pens, pencils, paper, and notebooks.

MATHEMATICS

Josh doesn't like arithmetic but does it fairly well; Ethan both likes it and is good at it; Caleb occasionally likes it but has his bored moments. We're presently using Mortensen Math workbooks and manipulatives for all three boys. Areas covered by the Mortensen program include arithmetic, algebra, calculus, measurement, and problem-solving. For Josh and Ethan, we're supplementing the Mortensen materials with the Stephen Hake worksheet series. For Caleb, we're using the Miquon workbooks from Key Curriculum Press, which have lots of clever little math puzzles and are generally more appealing than the Mortensen books. These can generally be used with the Mortensen manipulatives, though are designed for use with Cuisenaire rods, a set of which we also have.

We also plan to continue using math as much as possible in other academic disciplines and in daily life: graphing the results of science experiments, for example, or using measurements in carpentry and cooking projects.

Math resources: Mortensen manipulatives and workbooks, Stephen Hake worksheets, Miquon workbooks, Cuisenaire rods, base ten blocks, math games of various kinds, "Math Blaster" and "Math Rabbit" computer software, measuring and weighing apparatus, hand calculators, and various children's math project books, among them *Family Math* (Stenmark, Thompson, and Cossey) from the Lawrence Hall of Science and Marilyn Burns's *A Collection of Math Lessons* series, *I Hate Mathematics!*, and *Math for Smarty Pants*.

History/Geography

History and science are perhaps the crux of our curriculum, since historical or scientific topics are most frequently used as our central starting points. This year, what with all the new field trip possibilities in the Massachusetts area, we plan to concentrate on American history. We also plan to continue our map studies—interest in maps picked up this summer when we drove from Colorado to Massachusetts, map-reading all the way.

History/geography resources: Many historical and multicultural books, reference books, and activity books, among them *The Children's Picture Atlas, The Facts on File Children's Atlas, The Book of Where: Or How to Be Naturally Geographic* (Bell), *Windows to the World* and *More Windows to the World* (Everix), a subscription to *Faces* magazine, a children's periodical about world cultures, a globe-making kit, a set of National Geographic maps, several map puzzles, geography games, compasses, American history card and lotto games, a wall-size timeline, and many local historical sites to visit.

Science

We do a large amount of science reading and complete science projects of various kinds two to three times weekly. We do not use a formal science program, but some of our more frequently used resources are listed below. We acquired an excellent binocular microscope a few months ago, which we plan to use extensively this year.

Science resources: Many informational and activity books, including *The Backyard Scientist* series (Hoffmann), *The Way Things Work* (Macauley), the Brown Paper School Books science books, Eyewitness books, and as many books in the Let's-Read-and-Find-Out Science series as we've been able to lay our hands on. Other resources include a telescope, constellation finder, home planetarium, and star maps, a binocular microscope, miscellaneous chemistry equipment, two electricity/electronics project kits, shell and rock collections, various building sets, bug-collecting equipment, dissecting pans and instruments, several science games, and two parents, both of whom have Ph.D.s in cell biology/biochemistry.

Art/Music

In the past we have participated in a number of art classes, taught at various artists' organizations, galleries, or local art museums; we hope to locate similar classes or programs this year. At home, art is a near-daily activity: the boys paint and draw, model with clay, and build with various materials. We subscribe to *KidsArt,* a children's art magazine, and are frequent gallery and museum visitors.

Music is stickier for us, since the boys have a notably nonmusical mother. We listen to music of various kinds, and the boys all have recorders and beginning recorder books, with which they are learning to play. We have recently joined a weekly children's singing group.

Art/music resources: Several kinds of paints, pastels, markers and colored pencils, clay, instant papier-mâché, linoleum blocks, inks, brayers, and cutting tools, carpentry tools and wood scraps, a small loom, assorted picture-book biographies of artists, a collection of art postcards, art activity books including *Drawing With Children* (Mona Brookes) and *Mommy, It's a Renoir!* (Aline Wolf), a varied music collection including the *Music Masters* cassette tape series (biographies and musical selections of many famous composers), musical games, recorders and instruction books, a small piano keyboard, three harmonicas, and a father who can sing.

Physical Education

The boys are active. They play outside almost daily—which involves lots of running, jumping, and bike riding—and they do indoor aerobics, using a children's exercise videotape. In the past, they have taken swimming lessons and gymnastics, both of which we hope to continue.

Homeschool Curriculum 1997–1998

Joshua S. Rupp (approximately 10th/11th grade)
Ethan S. Rupp (approximately 9th/10th grade)
Caleb B. Rupp (approximately 8th/9th grade)

The boys, now all teenagers, pursue the bulk of their academic work independently, with help and review on a daily basis as needed/wanted, plus a good deal of discussion about what they've learned. All are becomingly increasingly specialized in their interests, though all still continue to study—with varying degrees of enthusiasm—the full range of academic basics. Joshua strongly prefers literature and writing to all else; Ethan just as strongly gravitates to the physical sciences and math; Caleb prefers literature, ancient history, and music.

LANGUAGE ARTS

Josh (sixteen) pursues a challenging reading program of his own, maintaining a record of completed books. Present favorite authors include Alexander Solzhenitsyn, Vladimir Nabokov, Yukio Mishima, Chaim Potok, Bernard Malamud, and Jorge Luis Borges. His reading habits are wide-ranging and varied, covering classical and modern writers, novels, autobiographies, essays, poetry, and plays. His stated intention is to educate himself through reading, which he certainly seems to be doing.

He also writes daily, fluently, and well, producing a growing body of work including short stories, essays, poems, plays, and (in progress) assorted novels.

He is taking a creative writing course in the fall semester at the local community college.

Ethan (fourteen) reads only technical books voluntarily, plus some science fiction. To encourage him to branch out a bit more, we plan to use assorted short story and essay collections, among them the *Reading and Understanding Short Stories* volumes in the Jamestown Literature Program, which include works by such authors as Sir Arthur Conan Doyle, Ray Bradbury, Kurt Vonnegut, Leo Tolstoy, and Saki.

Ethan has an excellent vocabulary but poor spelling and grammar skills; we plan to work on the latter through daily writing exercises, primarily essays and reports summarizing his science studies. Ethan also keeps up a frequent correspondence with two adult pen pals, one a physicist at Cornell, the other an independent computer specialist and graphics artist. These weekly or near-weekly letters, though intended on Ethan's part to further his science education, also allow him to hone his writing abilities.

Caleb (thirteen) reads continually, preferably modern fiction, science fiction, and fantasies. We plan to encourage him to try more varied genres, using a suggested reading list, plus the Jamestown Literature Program (see above) and the Introduction to the Great Books Series. He has already started book number one on the suggested reading list—George Orwell's *Animal Farm*—and says it's terrific.

Caleb writes well, though could improve his grammar skills somewhat. We plan to work on these through daily writing practice, including letters, creative writing projects, journal entries, and reports summarizing his other academic studies.

MATHEMATICS

Josh, who continues to dislike mathematics, will be reviewing algebra and studying geometry this year, using *Basic College Mathematics* (Charles D. Miller, Stanley A. Salzman, and Diana L. Hestwood) and *Geometry* (Harold Jacobs). We plan to supplement his math studies with assorted popular science/math books, such as *A Mathematician Reads the Newspaper* (John Paulos) and *Mathematical Scandals* (Theoni Pappas).

Ethan will be studying algebra and trigonometry, using *Elementary Algebra* (Harold Jacobs), *Basic College Mathematics*, *Trigonometry the Easy Way* (Douglas Downing), and whatever else he needs in the way of math texts; we plan to add over the course of the year. Ethan is a very self-motivated mathematical learner, since he uses math intensively in his physics and chemistry studies.

Caleb will be studying algebra using *Elementary Algebra*.

HISTORY/GEOGRAPHY

Joshua will continue his studies of both American and world history, using a varied assortment of books, history magazines, and journal articles. Sample materials include *American Lives* (Willard Sterne Randall and Nancy Nahra), *Readings in American Government* (Frank Bryan), *Don't Know Much Geography* (Kenneth Davis), and the Annual Editions *World History* and *American History* volumes.

Ethan, who deems all history useless, will continue to read Joy Hakim's *A History of US* American history series.

Caleb is also reading Hakim's *A History of US,* along with assorted books and magazines on archaeology and ancient history. (He subscribes, for example, to *Archaeology Magazine.*)

All three boys will be watching a variety of history video programs and miniseries, as well as the thirty-lesson video high-school-level world history lecture series by Lin Thompson ("World History") from the Teaching Company.

SCIENCE

Josh plans to study biology this year, using a variety of texts, science essay collections, and journal articles, among them *Biology* (Cecie Starr and Ralph Taggart). We have a number of experimental projects lined up, among them raising fruit flies and studying patterns of genetic inheritance, using the "Wisconsin Fast Plants" botany program, and learning how to prepare specimens for microscopic study. Josh will also be accessing biology tutorials and Web sites on the Internet and using biology computer software programs.

He will also be taking a class in bioethics at the local community college.

Ethan plans to continue his physics and chemistry studies, using *Physics* (John Saxon) and *Chemistry: Principles and Practice* (Daniel Reger, Scott Goode, and Edward Mercer). He is also teaching himself astronomy, using *Astronomy* (Eric Chaissen); computer programming; and electronics. He is extremely disciplined about his science studies, pursuing each subject daily, supplementing his texts with science essays, magazine and journal articles, discussion with his physicist pen pal at Cornell, on-line tutorials and information, and computer software. He has also set up an extensive chemistry lab in the basement.

Caleb has yet to zero in on a scientific discipline that he wants to study intensively. This year we plan to expose him to a range of topics through science essay collections and journal articles. He also plans to study astronomy, using assorted books, among them Chet Raymo's *365 Starry Nights,* plus star charts, binoculars, and telescope. He will also participate in biology and chemistry experiments with his brothers.

ART/MUSIC

The boys will continue their pottery work, in hopes of starting their own small pottery business. They will be helped toward this end by a mentor, a professional potter.

Josh plans to participate in the after-school art program for teenagers at the Vermont Arts Exchange. He will also be taking weekly piano lessons.

Ethan will be taking weekly violin lessons and will be participating in the Green Mountain Youth Orchestra.

Caleb will be taking weekly violin and piano lessons and will be participating in the Green Mountain Youth Orchestra.

All three boys will use assorted books and audiovisual resources to study art and music history. We will continue our frequent visits to art galleries and plan to attend local symphony and chamber music performances.

PHYSICAL EDUCATION

The boys routinely jog, hike, and bike in snowless seasons; this winter they plan to skate twice a week at the local rink and to participate in the homeschool downhill ski program. They also cross-country ski, swim, canoe, hoe the garden, mow the lawn and fields, shovel snow, and move heavy furniture for their mother.

Homeschooling how-tos, clearly, are highly individual, a matter of discovering what best suits the unique needs of your child. Initially this may be a bumpy process of trial and error, which gradually smooths out as you—the teaching parents—discover the ins and outs of your child's learning style. Homeschooling, like parenting itself, comes with a potential battery of stresses, problems, and worries. Many parents fall prey to unrealistic expectations, having formed a rosy mental picture of home education in which peaceful cooperative children cluster around the kitchen table, happily doing long division problems. This, of course, sometimes happens—and sometimes doesn't.

◆ **October 3, 1989**

A dreadful morning. First Ethan in an evil mood; then Ethan fighting with both of his brothers; then Josh and Caleb, ditto. Had planned to start camel projects today (this is the anniversary of the first camel imported into the United States) using home-written activity books. This started out cheerfully enough with everybody drawing camel pictures based on a color art print of a camel statue from the St. Louis Art Museum. Ethan, dissatisfied with his camel, got furious, tore his picture up, and threw his pencil, which hit

Caleb in the head; Caleb howled; Ethan told him—a forbidden phrase—to shut up. Caleb repeatedly jiggled Josh's elbow, which annoyed Joshua, and then spilled apple juice on Joshua's camel, which infuriated Joshua; and all went rapidly downhill from there. I dropped all thought of "school" and took everybody out for a long, long walk.

Over lunch, we read "How the Camel Got His Hump" and "The Elephant's Child" in Kipling's Just-So Stories, *after which Josh read "The Cat Who Walked by Himself" to himself.*

The boys spent the rest of the day building tents and forts in the living room, with chairs, broomsticks, clothesline, and blankets; also played computer games, made rubber-stamp pictures, and played chess.

Many of the stresses of homeschooling occur when parents—many of us understandably nervous when it comes to the education of our offspring—overreact to daily disasters. Sometimes kids bicker; sometimes they get bored; sometimes learning simply does not progress as expected. Sometimes one's beautifully planned unit study fails to catch the children's interest; you find yourself snapping at an increasingly rambunctious audience to sit up and pay attention; tempers—on both sides—fray; and learning goes down the tubes. One of the most difficult lessons that I've had to learn in homeschool is when to stop, to let go, to drop a project cold. It's dazzlingly clear when learning is taking place in a homeschool setting. Kids ask question after question (sometimes interrupting each other, which provides the alert parent with opportunities for etiquette training and socialization), bubble with suggestions, plunge into independent experiments, dash to the bookcases to find relevant books, and discuss their day's learning experience at great and informed length at the dinner table. It's equally clear when learning is *not* taking place: they're resentfully kicking the legs of their chairs, whining, asking annoyingly irrelevant questions ("Can we go outside now?"), and generally signaling that this is not the time, place, or topic to encourage intellectual growth. A major advantage of homeschooling is the freedom to deal with just this situation. You can quit then and there and do something else.

Another source of homeschool stress is the necessary commitment of parental time. Homeschooling is a rewarding but time-consuming process, potentially expanding—like housework—to fill every available hour of the day. Some homeschooling parents, asked how much time they spend daily in homeschool pursuits, answered: "twenty-four hours times seven! We truly are always doing one thing or another and feel that the children are always learning." "All the time. Our children's learning is inseparable from the rest of their lives." "Every minute that the kids are home and awake." This is both a joyous and an overwhelming prospect; a recurrent complaint among teaching parents at support group meetings is the need for more personal time.

The amount of time that children spend learning, however, and the amount of monitored time spent in conventional academic pursuits are two wholly different things. When our sons were of elementary and middle school age, we generally reserved three or four hours a day—usually in the mornings—for directed studies, projects, and academic exercises. During this time, the kids knew that they could have full parental attention. We also read together frequently—always during lunch and for an hour or so at bedtime—and we went on weekly field trips. Now that the boys are of high school age, they manage their time for themselves, asking for help and direction as necessary—generally about an hour per kid per day. "Educational time," however, is difficult to define in the open milieu of homeschooling. Is a joint bread-baking session "school"? An afternoon of conversation and potato planting in the backyard garden or wallpapering the kitchen? A day spent lying on the couch, absorbed in *The Hobbit* or *The Witch of Blackbird Pond*?

And again, it's also important to remember that kids need time to themselves. Children need time to daydream, to exercise their imaginations, to pursue their own activities, to read and write as they please. Learning is a complex process, and in our eagerness to provide kids with adequate input and stimulation, it's easy to overlook their need for downtime. Kids need relaxed periods in which to assimilate new information, to construct and enhance their personal mental frameworks.

◆ **August 15, 1991**

Pressured by deadlines, I have done nothing with the boys for days, other than read to them at bedtime. Learning, however, has proceeded perfectly well in my absence. The boys have spent a lot of time building wonderful little working machines with their Lego Dacta kits, including a helicopter, windmill, drill, crane, windshield wiper, and motorized truck. They collaborated on making a vast bug collection, each specimen carefully preserved in a test tube in some mysterious glop from their chemistry set, examined by magnifying glass with repeated reference to insect field guides, identified, and labeled. They built and painted a trio of dinosaur models, and Ethan is working on an enormous airplane model, a replica of the Blackbird. Josh read Mossflower *(Brian Jacques),* Kneeknock Rise *(Natalie Babbitt),* The Little Prince *(Antoine de Saint-Exupery), and* The House With the Clock in its Walls *(John Bellairs); Ethan read* The Woodshed Mystery *in the Boxcar Children series (Gertrude Chandler Warner); and Caleb read a stack of Berenstain Bear books (Jan and Stan Berenstain). Josh wrote steadily, turning out many short stories and poems. (He has decided, he says, to be a writer and an entomologist when he grows up.) Ethan has also started a story notebook, now stuffed with short stories in which he bravely tackles words like* porcupine *and* galaxy.

The boys played several rounds of "Space Hop," an astronomical board game, "O Euclid," a geometry card game, and several computer games. They weeded and watered the garden. They watched Robin Hood *(starring Errol Flynn) and* The Man in the Iron Mask *(starring Richard Chamberlain) on videotape. They spent hours modeling with Fimo clay and baking their creations in the oven: they now have an entire collection of baked-clay knights, horses, and dragons. They built block castles. They went swimming with friends. Their father began teaching them to play tennis.*

As well as time spent directly playing, learning, and interacting with your children, homeschool generally requires some preparation time. Our children's education, we found, proceeded most smoothly when (more or less) organized. To ensure this, Randy and I devoted considerable time to homeschool preparation: mapping out (approximate) weekly and monthly schedules, accumulating resources and appropriate books, writing activity books and—later—assignment lists. If we skimped too much on this, we found, homeschool often disintegrated into frustration, disappointment, and chaos: a crucial ingredient was lacking for a planned science experiment; the art gallery, when we arrived, armed with pencils and sketchbooks, was closed on Wednesdays; we were out of construction paper or glue; or we lacked adequate books on the moon, the spider, or the classification of clouds. Homeschool is inevitably a balancing act between flexibility and structure; and too little of either leads to trouble. Plan ahead.

And finally: relax. Homeschooling works. Children, given the freedom to learn, do.

All men by nature desire to know.

ARISTOTLE
METAPHYSICS

RESOURCES

BOOKS

Creative Projects for Independent Learners.
Banks, Janet Caudill; CATS Publications, 1995.
A curriculum guide for kids in grades 3–8, filled with creative projects for them to tackle on their own or in small groups.

Family Learning: How to Help Your Children Succeed in School by Learning at Home.
Russell, William F.; First World, 1997.
A large collection of activities, games, discussion suggestions, and hands-on projects in all academic subjects.

Frames of Mind: The Theory of Multiple Intelligences.
Gardner, Howard; Basic Books, 1993.
Intelligence, explains scientist Howard Gardner, consists of several major components, which each individual possesses in different degrees. An individual's predominant form of intelligence—for example, linguistic, logical-mathematical, musical, or bodily-kinesthetic—influences his/her preferred learning style.

Homeschooling: A Patchwork of Days.
Lande, Nancy; WindyCreek Press, 1996.
Descriptions of a "typical day" in the lives of 30 homeschooling families.

The Homeschool Reader.
Hegener, Mark and Helen, eds.; Home Education Press, 1995.
A collection of articles from *Home Education Magazine*, including general information on homeschooling and many descriptions of home teaching methods, ideas, and projects in many academic subjects.

How to Write a Low-Cost/No-Cost Curriculum for Your Home-School Child.
Hendrickson, Borg; Mountain Meadow Press, 1995.
How to write a curriculum for kids of all ages, with helpful worksheets and lists of typical grade-level requirements.

In Their Own Way.
Armstrong, Thomas; J. P. Tarcher, 1988.
Using Howard Gardner's theory of multiple intelligences (see below), Armstrong proposes techniques for identifying your child's individual learning style and suggests approaches for maximizing learning.

Parents Are Teachers, Too.
Jones, Claudia; Williamson Publishing, 1988.
Advice for effective participation in your children's education, with many teaching and activity suggestions for kids aged 3–12.

Raising Lifelong Learners: A Parent's Guide.
Bellino, Lydia, and Lucy McCormick Calkins; Addison-Wesley, 1997.
Many suggestions for encouraging young children to become independent learners.

The Successful Homeschool Family Handbook.
Moore, Raymond and Dorothy; Thomas Nelson Publishers, 1994.
Homeschooling how-tos and advice from Raymond and Dorothy Moore, the "grandparents of modern homeschooling." Includes many accounts of the problems and situations encountered by different homeschooling families. Christian orientation.

Trust the Children: An Activity Guide for Homeschooling and Alternative Learning.
Kealoha, Anna; Celestial Arts, 1995.
Creative games, projects, activities, and teaching techniques in all academic subjects.

The Unschooling Handbook: How to Use the Whole World as Your Child's Classroom.
Griffith, Mary; Prima Publishing, 1998.
An explanation of the natural learning process called "unschooling," with many suggestions for an unschooled education.

CURRICULUM SOURCES

Calvert School
105 Tuscany Rd.
Baltimore, MD 21210
(410) 243-6030
fax (410) 366-0674
Web site: www.jhu.edu/~calvert
Complete correspondence courses for kids in grades K–8, including all teachers' manuals, texts, workbooks, and supplementary materials. Some courses and materials are available separately.

Clonlara School Home Based Education Program
1289 Jewett St.
Ann Arbor, MI 48104
(313) 769-4515
Web site: www.clonlara.org
Creative grade-appropriate curricula and many support services for homeschooled students in grades K–12.

Curriculum by Grade and Subject
Web site:
www.e-bus.com/curricul.htm
Click on appropriate grade and academic subject for a list of school-sanctioned requirements.

Curriculum Services
26801 Pine Ave.
Bonita Springs, FL 34135
(941) 992-6381
fax (941) 992-6473
Complete educational programs for kids in grades K–12 covering all subjects required by the public schools and using public school materials.

Oak Meadow School
Box 740
Putney, VT 05346
(802) 387-2021
fax (802) 387-5108
Web site: www.oakmeadow.com
Integrative learning programs for kids in grades K–12. There are several enrollment options. Complete curriculum packages include all books, workbooks, lesson plans, and supplementary materials.

The Sycamore Tree Center for Home Education
2179 Meyer Pl.
Costa Mesa, CA 92627
information (949) 650-4466
e-mail:
75767.1417@compuserve.com
Web site: www.sycamoretree.com
Bible-based or secular study programs for grades K–12.

TRISMS
5710 E. 63rd Pl.
Tulsa, OK 74136
(918) 585-2778 or (918) 491-6826
Web site: www.trisms.com
History-centered curricula for kids in grades 6–12.

Upattinas School and Resource Center
429 Greenridge Rd.
Glenmore, PA 19343
(610) 458-5138
Web site:
www.chesco.com/upattinas
Offers an Independent Home Program for homeschoolers. Individual curriculum packets are available for each academic subject.

Unschooling Sources

F.U.N. News
1688 Belhaven Woods Ct.
Pasadena, MD 21122-3727
voice mail/fax: (410) 360-7330
e-mail: FUNNews@MCImail.com
A quarterly newsletter for unschoolers.
    4 issues/$8

Family Unschoolers Network
Web site: iqcweb.com/fun/
FAQs, information, resources, and a message board for unschoolers.

The Libertarian Unschooling Page of Nemesis Eudaimonos
Web site:
www.geocities.com/Athens/6529
Essays, articles, and general information on the philosophy and practice of unschooling.

Unit Study Sources

Abecedarius
Bookwork
3439 NE Alameda St.
Portland, OR 97212
Web site: www.icsn.com/bookwork/
Unit studies for kids aged 5 to 7. Each themed study includes a versatile combination of projects, activities, fiction and nonfiction books, and relevant Web sites. Available in print versions or by on-line subscription.

Amanda Bennett's Unit Study Adventures
e-mail: Amanda@unitstudy.com
Web site: www.unitstudy.com
Ready-to-use lesson plans for unit studies, each containing five to six

weeks of learning activities for kids of all ages (preK–grade 12). Each themed unit study uses a range of multidisciplinary approaches. The plans are written from a Christian perspective.

Guided Educational Tours

Box 658
Three Lakes, WI 54562-0658
Web site: www.newnorth.net/get/
Themed unit studies for kids of all ages, centering around guided explorations of relevant Web sites.

KONOS, Inc.

Box 250
Anna, TX 75409
(972) 924-2712
fax: (972) 924-2733
Web site: www.konos.com
A large and detailed collection of unit studies assembled in the form of a three-volume curriculum, which is written from a Christian perspective.

Unit Studies at the Mining Company

Web site:
homeschooling.miningco.com/library/materials/blUnits.htm
On-line unit study sources.

Unit Study Resource Station

Web site: home.gvi.net/~hsunits
An on-line resource for home-schoolers creating their own unit studies. Users can research a specific subject to find related books, videos, field trips, computer software, and activities.

The Village Learning Center Program

Web site:
www.snowcrest.net/villcen/wvlc.html
A unit-study approach to high school.

6

TOOLS OF THE TRADE

I cannot live without books.

THOMAS JEFFERSON

Experience is the child of Thought, and Thought is the child of Action. We cannot learn men from books.

BENJAMIN DISRAELI

Most families already possess the basic equipment to stock a homeschool. If you've got kids, chances are you already have reams of paper (lined, unlined, and colored), pens, pencils, and felt-tip markers, paints and crayons, erasers, scissors, and glue, modeling materials, cooking utensils, a clock, a calendar, a library card, and a lot of imagination. From these rock-bottom beginnings, homeschool tools vary with the needs of the students. One family's essentials—basketball hoop, binoculars, piano keyboard—may be another family's waste of money and time. Some general resources that we've found useful follow.

BOOKS, BOOKS, BOOKS...AND A LIBRARY CARD

The public library is an excellent source of resources for homeschoolers, providing books, magazines, reference works, music selections and videos, and literary programs for persons of all ages, from story hours for small fry to book discussion groups for teenagers and adults. Most librarians are delighted to help information-seeking students with reading suggestions and helpful instruction on ways to conduct library research. Many libraries—if you desperately need something they lack—will track down books for you via interlibrary loans; and libraries, unlike bookstores, stock both recent publications and wonderful but sadly out-of-print books. Since the library is so heavily frequented by most homeschoolers, it's also an excellent place to connect with like-minded peers. Consider posting a support group notice on the library bulletin board.

Library book sales—many libraries hold these annually—are excellent and inexpensive sources of books, magazines, and maps.

A Filing System

Homeschooling generates overwhelming amounts of paper. Each year we accumulate towering stacks of kids' artwork, math papers, short stories, history reports, scientific observations, records, and experimental notes, reading lists, and foreign language worksheets. We store these in cardboard cartons in colored file folders (labeled by year, subject, and child's name). If we ever need to produce evidence of educational activity, there it sits, neatly labeled: Ethan/Math/1993.

A Tabletop Copy Machine

We have a secondhand model, acquired ten years ago; new versions of the same ilk now start around $700. One of the boys, at some point in the distant past, broke off its attached paper tray; its upper cover is secured with duct tape; and periodically, while in action, it makes an ominous grating sound. Still, it works, and it's worth its weight in gold. We use it almost daily, copying worksheets, maps, assignment forms, useful magazine articles, records, fact sheets, and supplementary reading materials. It has enabled us—innumerable times—to transform one student's worth of materials into three. I figure it has more than paid for itself.

Computer/Access to the Internet

While the jury is still out—and vociferously arguing—over the educational benefits of the computer, we have found the Internet to be an unparalleled homeschool resource. A mind-boggling range of information is available on-line: science and math tutorials; planetariums; maps of all kinds; dictionaries (English and foreign-language); encyclopedias; virtual tours of historical sites, museums, and art galleries; timelines; biographies of famous persons, past and present; art projects; the full texts of classic works of literature. Users can visit Monticello, view the launching of the space shuttle, check on growing world population statistics, build and operate a robot, read *Hamlet,* and get help with their algebra homework.

Games

Among the proposals for "new education" put forth by Neil Postman and Charles Weingartner in *Teaching as a Subversive Activity* (see page 10) is a suggestion for a "games curriculum." Games, the authors explain, generate "a learning environment that is much more congruent to what we know about learning than any other approach now used in schools." Games eliminate the need for an authoritarian teacher—in games, the teacher at most acts as an adviser or coach—and, depending on what you choose to play, games develop a range of thinking strategies, skills, and concepts. Many different kinds of informational, educational, and strategy games are available commercially. Kids also enjoy designing and playing their own.

An Arizona homeschooling mother writes: "This week's math consisted of one very long 'Monopoly' game, which has still not ended. At this point, John is a very very rich land baron; Jason is holding his own with several hotels and a moderate bank account; and I am in the poorhouse, taking loans from John. The kids are counting, planning their financing, making change with ease, buying and trading, learning about taxes and other financial obligations, as well as title deeds, monopolies, mortgages, and probability. I have made sure during the game that they had to use the various math functions, so at this point I see no need for math books or drill every day..."

SOURCES FOR GAMES

Aristoplay, Ltd.
450 S. Wagner Rd.
Ann Arbor, MI 48107
(888) GR8-GAME
fax (734) 995-4611
Web site: www.aristoplay.com

Chatham Hill Games
Box 253
Chatham, NY 12037
(518) 392-5022
(800) 554-3039
fax (518) 392-3121
Web site: www.ragionnet.com/
colberk/chgames.html

Turn Off the TV
Box 4162
Bellevue, WA 98009
(800) 949-8688
fax (425) 588-7564
Web site: www.turnoffthetv.com

U.S. Chess Federation
3054 NYS Rte. 9W
New Windsor, NY 12553
(914) 562-8350
Web site: www.uschess.org

Wff'n Proof Learning Games
1490 South Blvd.
Ann Arbor, MI 48104
(313) 665-2269

Worldwide Games
Box 517
Colchester, CT 06415-0517
(800) 888-0987
fax (800) 566-6678
Web site:
www.worldwidegames.com

OLD MACHINES

Never throw anything away. Our boys, over the years, have disassembled and (sometimes) reassembled an education-rich collection of dysfunctional machines, among them defunct coffeepots, clocks, electric mixers, toasters, blenders, telephones, bicycles, lamps, typewriters, computers, and lawn mowers. The proprietor of our local music shop gave them a full-size electronic piano keyboard that had been damaged during shipping: fifteen minutes with a screwdriver and a pair of wire clippers gave the boys a functional piano (with an immense array of interesting musical accoutrements).

STORY ENVELOPE

Our story envelope is a fat manila envelope, stuffed with postcards, photographs, and pictures clipped from magazines. Each was chosen for its storytelling potential. A random handful turns up an art postcard of a Grandma Moses snow scene, pictures of dinosaurs, kangaroos, the Horsehead Nebula, and a castle on the Rhine, and a photograph—taken by me at a Renaissance Fair—of a knight in armor on horseback. We used these repeatedly for years—some are ragged—first for oral storytelling sessions, later as story starters for creative writing.

ART BOX

Art is everywhere, and a lot of it is recyclable. When the boys were younger, we kept a pair of large cartons in the basement in which we stored the raw materials for art and building projects: boxes of all kinds, from shoe and cereal boxes to tiny jewelry-size boxes, egg and milk cartons, paper-towel tubes, corks, bottle caps, colored foils, bubble wrap, wood scraps. The boys used these—plus a lot of glue, tape, and poster paint—to build everything from medieval castles to puppet theaters to spaceships to massive abstract sculptures. We filled a smaller container with stickers, gift paper scraps, sequins, beads, buttons, yarn, dried beans, and snippets of felt and fabric, for making collages.

REFERENCE BOOKS

A dictionary, an encyclopedia, an atlas, field identification guides, *The Guinness Book of World Records,* a biographical dictionary.

Other homeschool essentials, necessities, and near-indispensable conveniences include:

BOOKSHELVES/BOOKCASES

The accumulation of books, books, and more books implies someplace to store them. Every year, it seems, we build another wall or so of bookshelves, a project that not only provides needed literary storage space but also enhances mathematical and carpentry skills. The one problem: we're running out of walls.

TELEVISION/VCR

Like the computer, it's all in how you use it: TV generates mindless cartoons, gratuitous violence, celebrity gossip, kid-luring commercials, and *Dukes of Hazzard* reruns; it also offers historical documentaries, science programs, *Reading Rainbow,* and excellent National Geographic specials. A wealth of superb educational material is also available on videotape.

SOURCES

Discovery Channel Multimedia
Box 1089
Florence, KY 41022
(800) 678-3343
Web site: www.discovery.com
Video titles from programs and series aired on the Discovery Channel.

Movies Unlimited
3015 Darnell Rd.
Philadelphia, PA 19154
(800) 4-MOVIES or (215) 637-4444
e-mail:
movies@moviesunlimited.com
Web site:
www.moviesunlimited.com
Over 40,000 video titles of all kinds, reasonably priced. The massive catalog costs $11.95, but it's worth it.

PBS Home Video
1320 Braddock Pl.
Alexandria, VA 22314-1698
(800) 645-4PBS
Web site: www.pbs.org
Video titles from PBS on a wide range of subjects.

Schoolmasters Video
745 State Circle, Box 1941
Ann Arbor, MI 48106
(800) 521-2832
Web site: www.school-tech.com
Hundreds of educational videos for kids in grades K–9.

The Teaching Company
7405 Alban Station Ct.
Suite A107
Springfield, VA 22150-2318
(800) 832-2412

High school– and college-level courses on videotapes and audiocassettes.

Zenger Media
10200 Jefferson Blvd., Box 802
Culver City, CA 90232-0802
(800) 421-4246 or
(310) 839-2436
fax (800) 944-5432 or
(310) 839-2249
e-mail: access@ZengerMedia.com
Web site:
ZengerMedia.com/Zenger
A 250-plus-page catalog of educational videos and CD-ROMs for grades 4 and up in the fields of history, geography, government, science, and the humanities.

Audiocassette/CD Player

For listening to music, stories, plays, and books on tape, and to recorded lecture series. And if you need more reasons to listen, consider the phenomenon now referred to as "the Mozart effect": recent studies have indicated that kids exposed to complex classical music—as little as ten minutes per day—show significant increases in spatial-temporal reasoning abilities, reading skills, and general intelligence.

For books on tape, see page 129; for music sources, page 142.

Index Cards

We use these continually. In our hands, they've been transformed into illustrated flash cards, geography and math games, story-starter cards, "Trivial Pursuit"–style question cards, personal vocabulary cards, and a truly creative collection of kid-made flip books.

Rolls of Plain Brown Paper

Again, used by us for a wide range of educational purposes, among them making timelines, maps, and murals, tracing kids' bodies for anatomy diagrams, and many art projects.

It doesn't take much to buy a roll of brown paper, but selecting teaching materials and specific educational resources is always a tricky business. It is often difficult to predict in advance what will most appeal to your child; and often materials that were wildly successful with one kid will prove dismally ineffective with another. To avoid expensive educational failures, it's best when possible to preview proposed materials. Several books that give detailed reviews of educational resources are available.

The Big Book of Home Learning: Preschool and Elementary/Teen and Adult/Afterschooling.
Pride, Mary; Crossway Books, 1998.

The Complete Home Learning Source Book.
Rupp, Rebecca; Crown, 1998.

Family Learning: How to Help Your Children Succeed in School by Learning at Home.
Russell, William F.; First World, 1997.

Home Education Resource Guide.
Gorder, Cheryl; Blue Bird Publishing, 1996.

The Home School Source Book.
Reed, Donn; Brook Farm Books, 1991.

READING

The first hurdle that most young learners face is that of learning to read. Reading is such an essential skill that an entire academic discipline has grown up around it: there are reading specialists, reading seminars, professional journals devoted to reading, and book after book about the theory and practice of learning to read. The most common buzzwords in the world of early reading are *phonics* and *whole language,* opposing philosophies and methodologies between which public school classrooms have seesawed for decades. Generally, phonics proponents advocate the sequential teaching of single letter sounds, letter combinations, and finally whole words, showing children how to "sound out" unfamiliar words letter by letter. "Whole language" fans encourage whole-word recognition, in which children decipher new words through a mixture of memory and logical guess, based on context.

While a few phonics-based readers manage to maintain a clever story line with nothing but three-letter short-*a* words, most sacrifice content to function, which means that any excitement comes from the act of reading something (anything), not from the nature of what is read. "The rag man pats the ram" may (or may not) turn your child on to the joys of literature. Whole-language supporters prefer literature-based reading programs, in which kids learn to read through the medium of real books. Two of our children, after early childhoods of intensive and continual reading aloud, simply learned to read on their own, using—apparently—a largely whole-language approach; the third, a late reader, studied phonics. The commonsense approach seems to be a combination of the two, as best suits your particular child, with lots of companionable group reading in between.

Along with *how* to read comes the question of *what* to read—about which each child, as soon as he or she is old enough to toddle to the bookshelves, will have strong opinions of his/her own. Excellent sources for parents attempting to encourage a varied and high-quality reading program are collections of annotated book lists (see below). These generally include basic information about each book (title, author, publisher), a plot summary, an age recommendation, and—sometimes—a brief list of similar or related books. Many young readers enjoy a multifaceted approach to literature, in which favorite children's books are linked to arts and crafts activities, drama, music, cooking projects, science experiments, and the like. Make a batch of blueberry muffins, for example, to accompany a reading of Robert McCloskey's *Blueberries for Sal*; design and decorate a spectacular hat with Dr. Seuss's *The 500 Hats of Bartholomew Cubbins*; make your own illustrated bookmarks; try reading your way around the world, marking the location of each book on the world map.

READING RESOURCES

Any Child Can Read Better: Developing Your Child's Reading Skills Outside the Classroom.
Weiner, Harvey S.; Oxford University Press, 1996.
Activities, exercises, and suggestions for enhancing early reading skills.

Children Learning to Read: A Guide for Parents and Teachers.
Itzkoff, Seymour W.; Praeger Publishing, 1996.
A detailed discussion of the developmental stages of learning how to read, with accompanying explanations of the educational practices most appropriate to each stage. Itzkoff also includes a review of the phonics versus whole-language debate.

Games for Reading.
Kaye, Peggy; Pantheon Books, 1984.
Games and projects for early readers, variously covering sight vocabulary, phonics skills, and reading comprehension.

How to Stock a Home Library Inexpensively.
Williams, Jane; Bluestocking Press, 1995.
How to get the most our of your book budget, plus a large list of sources for low-priced books.

99 Ways to Get Kids to Love Reading.
Leonhardt, Mary; Three Rivers Press, 1997.
Solidly helpful hints for encouraging readers of all ages, from toddlers on up.

Annotated Book Lists

Best Books for Beginning Readers.
Gunning, Thomas G.; Allyn & Bacon, 1997.
A 250-plus-page bibliography of simple books for beginners.

Books Kids Will Sit Still For.
Freeman, Judy; R. R. Bowker, 1990; and *More Books Kids Will Sit Still For.* Freeman, Judy. R. R. Bowker, 1995.
Reviews of over 2,000 "kid-tested" books, categorized by age, for kids in K–6. The books include a very detailed subject index.

Creative Uses of Children's Literature.
Paulin, Mary Ann; Library Professional Publications, 1982.
An encyclopedic list of books for children of all ages, creatively linked by theme. Books can be grouped in any number of ways, Paulin explains, connected, for example, by author, subject, historical period, or literary genre. There's an equally valuable sequel, *More Creative Uses of Children's Literature* (Library Professional Publications, 1992).

Eyeopeners!
Kobrin, Beverly K.; Penguin Books, 1988; and *Eyeopeners II!* Scholastic, 1995.
Reviews of children's nonfiction books, listed by subject.

Magazines for Kids and Teens.
Stoll, Donald R., ed.; International Reading Association.
An annotated alphabetical listing of over 200 kids' magazines on every subject from French to world history to science.
International Reading Association
800 Barksdale Rd.
Box 8139
Newark, DE 19714-8139
(800) 336-READ, X266

Outstanding Books for the College Bound.
Lewis, Marjorie, ed.; American Library Association, 1996.
Over 1000 "outstanding" books for teenagers, arranged by genre.

The Read-Aloud Handbook.
Trelease, Jim; Penguin Books, 1995.
Why and how to read aloud, with a large annotated list of good books for young readers.

Book Catalogs

Chinaberry Books
2780 Via Orange Way, Suite B
Spring Valley, CA 91978
(619) 670-5200 or
(800) 776-2242

Great Books Foundation
35 E. Wacker Dr., Suite 2300
Chicago, IL 60601-2298
(800) 222-5870
Web site: www.greatbooks.org

Learning Links
2300 Marcus Ave.
New Hyde Park, NY 11042
(516) 437-9071 or
(800) 724-2616

Sundance
Box 1326
Littleton, MA 01460-9936
(800) 343-8204

Books and Stories on Tape

Audio Bookshelf
174 Prescott Hill Rd.
Northport, ME 04849
(800) 234-1713
e-mail: audbkshf@agate.net

Great Tapes for Kids
Box 954
Middlebury, VT 05753
(888) KID-TAPES
(802) 462-2623
Web site: www.greattapes.com

Greathall Productions
Box 5061
Charlottesville, VA 22905-5061
(804) 296-4288 or (800) 477-6234
fax (804) 296-4490
e-mail: greathall@greathall.com

Recorded Books, Inc.
270 Skipjack Rd.
Prince Frederick, MD 20678
(800) 638-1304
fax (410) 535-5499

Books On-line

Amazon Books
www.amazon.com

Barnes & Noble Booksellers
www.barnesandnoble.com

Bookwire Index to Children's Booksellers
www.bookwire.com

Just for Kids Children's Bookstore
www.just-for-kids.com

Powell's Books: New, Used, and Out-of-Print
www.powells.com

WRITING

Writing skills generally go hand-in-hand with beginning reading. Usually kids progress from manuscript handwriting—that is, printing, in gradually decreasing sizes as motor control improves—to cursive handwriting and, now that we've entered the computer age, keyboarding. Recommended tools for beginning writers include manuscript tablets with wide-ruled lines (in blue) with a red divider down the middle and either a nice fat pencil or a pencil grip, which is a little rubber attachment that slides over the end of a pencil, comfortably contoured for the better grasp of small fingers.

Writing in what my sons so chillingly call "the olden days" was strictly limited in its early years by the necessity for proper spelling, grammar, and punctuation—feats that were largely beyond most early beginners. In the 1980s, however, studies of children learning to write demonstrated the benefits of creative freedom. Kids, given their heads, plunged into challenging writing projects, inventing their own spellings, dealing as best they could with the complexities of grammar, and reveling in the freedom to write as they pleased.

Once kids are comfortable writing, the sky is the limit. Popular modern writing programs include "journaling" in which kids are encouraged to write every day in personal journals or diaries; and "writing across the curriculum" (WAC) programs, in which kids write in all academic subjects, including science, history, geography, art, and math. Such writing helps kids assimilate lesson material, as well as honing language ability. Examples include records of science experiments, descriptions of math problems and procedures, and summaries of history topics and discussions. Almost everybody's favorite, however, is creative writing: stories, poems, newsletters, novels, plays.

WRITING RESOURCES

Any Child Can Write: An At-Home Guide to Encouraging Your Child's Elementary Education.
Weiner, Harvey S.; Bantam, 1990.
Games, exercises, goals, and techniques for developing writers, from kindergarten through high school.

The Creative Journal for Children.
Capacchione, Lucia; Shambala, 1989.
Journaling for preschoolers to upper-elementary students, with many activity suggestions.

Families Writing.
Stillman, Peter R.; Calendar Islands, 1998.
Many suggestions for encouraging family writing, along with a lifetime of wonderful writing activities for persons of all ages. By the same author, also see **Write Away: A Friendly Guide for Teenage Writers** (Boyton/Cook, 1995).

Games for Writing: Playful Ways to Help Your Child Learn to Write.
Kaye, Peggy; Noonday Press, 1995.
Over 50 different writing games and activities for beginning writers in grades K–3.

GNYS AT WRK.
Bissex, Glenda; Harvard University Press, 1985.
A detailed account of a five-year-old learning to write, tracing his progress from the beginnings of invented spelling on up. (GNYS AT WRK = genius at work.)

If You're Trying to Teach Kids How to Write, You've Gotta Have This Book!
Frank, Marjorie; Incentive Publications, 1995.
A creative wealth of writing projects and activities for kids of all ages.

99 Ways to Get Kids to Love Writing.
Leonhardt, Mary; Three Rivers Press, 1998.
Suggestions, approaches, and activities for encouraging young writers.

Write From the Start.
Graves, Donald and Virginia Stuart; E. P. Dutton, 1985.
A detailed explanation of a writing program in which beginners "write from the start," using invented spelling.

Writing Because We Love To: Homeschoolers At Work.
Sheffer, Susannah; Heinemann, 1992.
How to be a supportive reader of your children's writing, with many examples.

WRITING CATALOGS

The Writing Company
10200 Jefferson Blvd.
Box 802
Culver City, CA 90232-0802
(310) 839-2436 or (800) 421-4246
Web site: www.writingco.com

Zaner-Bloser
2200 W. Fifth Ave.
Box 16764
Columbus, OH 43216-6764
(800) 421-3018
Web site: www.zaner-bloser.com

MATHEMATICS

Beginners, recent research indicates, do best when mathematical learning is concrete. The hands-on approach to math involves the use of what are collectively known as "math manipulatives": blocks, rods, counters, shapes, gadgets, and tools with which kids, through a directed process of experiment and play, learn mathematical concepts and operations. Among the best-known of math manipulatives are Cuisenaire rods, sets of richly colorful wooden or plastic blocks and rods, in graded sizes from one to ten, with which kids can learn everything from counting to fractions; and the similar Mortensen manipulatives, a collection of color-coded plastic bars sized from units to 100 squares, with accompanying workbooks.

As young learners progress, most homeschoolers supplement hands-on projects with workbooks or texts. Especially popular among homeschoolers are the Saxon math books (see Saxon Publishers, page 134), based on the "gently repetitious" learning method formally known as "incremental development." The Saxon books emphasize plenty of practice, a gradual presentation of new information, and a continual reiteration of learned concepts. The Saxon system is thorough and effective, though the presentation is flavorless and dull. Some children respond to it well—it works, and dedicated users can readily track their growing competence. Others (two of our boys, for example) find it off-putting. Luckily there are many alternatives (see Math Catalogs, page 134).

Popular approaches to math also include "real-world math" programs, in which kids are urged to learn math as it relates to their daily lives and to the world around them: for example, math in the supermarket, in the shopping mall, on the road, in the newspapers, in the kitchen, in sports. Kids thus learn to compute sales prices and gas mileage, calculate and compare cost per pound, interpret sports statistics, and—in the process of whipping up a batch of banana bread—discover principles of measurement, multiplication, and fractions. Many math concepts can be readily taught through games, of which there are many commercially available—among them such tried-and-true classics as backgammon and chess; or, if your children are bookworms, through literature. Many children's books emphasize—whether the kids realize it or not—mathematical thinking, from creative counting books through David Schwartz's *How Much Is a Million?* (Lothrop, Lee & Shepard, 1985), Demi's *One Grain of Rice: A Mathematical Folktale* (Scholastic, 1997), and Norton Juster's *The Phantom Tollbooth* (Alfred A. Knopf, 1961).

MATH RESOURCES

Family Math.
Stenmark, Jean Kerr, Virginia Thompson, and Ruth Cossey; Lawrence Hall of Science, 1986.
A large and varied collection of math activities for children aged 5–18 (and their parents). Each activity is accompanied by an explanation of its place in the academic mathematics curriculum, complete instructions, a grade recommendation, and suggestions for further supplementary projects. The book includes many reproducible master sheets, among them tangram patterns, blank fill-it-in-yourself calendar pages, graph paper in several grid sizes, coin boards, place value boards, and hundred charts.

How Math Works.
Vorderman, Carol; Reader's Digest, 1996.
Challenging and creative activities, mathematical information, and lots of color photographs. The book is an activity-based approach to many different subsets of mathematics, for kids aged 8–14.

Humble Pi: The Role Mathematics Should Play in American Education.
Smith, Michael K.; Prometheus Books, 1994.
A thoughtful book for adults on how math should be taught in schools. The author feels that many kids get more than they need, and suggests that math curricula be geared to individual needs and interests.

Mathematics Their Way.
Baratta-Lorton, Mary; Addison-Wesley, 1995.
A complete activity-centered mathematics program from children in grades K–2, with reproducible worksheets.

Math for the Very Young: A Handbook of Activities for Parents and Teachers.
Polansky, Lydia, ed.; John Wiley & Sons, 1995.
Creative activities, games, projects, crafts, songs, and fascinating facts to encourage mathematical thinking in preschool and primary grade kids.

Math Power: How to Help Your Child Love Math Even If You Don't.
Kenschaft, Patricia Clark; Addison-Wesley, 1997.
Methods for getting your children to enjoy math, using games and activities.

Math Wizardry for Kids.
Kenda, Margaret, and Phyllis S. Williams; Barron's, 1995.
A attractive 300-plus-page collection of projects, games, experiments, explanations, and information for mathematicians aged 7–12.

Read Any Good Math Lately? Children's Books for Mathematical Learning, K–6.
Whitin, David J., and Sandra Wilde; Heinemann, 1992.

An annotated list of popular children's books with mathematical themes, plus related project suggestions.

MATH CATALOGS

Cuisenaire Company of America
Box 5026
White Plains, NY 10602-5026
(800) 237-0338 or (800) 237-3142
Web site: www.cuisenaire-dsp.com

Delta Hands-On Math
Box 3000
Nashua, NH 03061-3000
(800) 442-5444
Web site: www.delta-ed.com

Institute for Math Mania
Box 910
Montpelier, VT 05601-0910

(802) 223-5871 or
(800) NUMERAL

Key Curriculum Press
Box 2304
Berkeley, CA 94702-0304
(800) 995-MATH
Web site: www.keypress.com

Mortensen Math Academic Excellence Institute
2450 Fort Union Blvd.
Salt Lake City, UT 84121
(801) 944-2500 or
(800) 338-9939
Web site: www.mortensenmath
direct.com

Saxon Publishers
1320 W. Lindsey St.
Norman, OK 73069
(800) 284-7019
Web site: www.saxonpub.com

SCIENCE

Science, in all its many permutations, is the academic subject most practicing and potential homeschoolers seem to worry the most about. "I hated science in school," writes a homeschooler from New York. "I took as few science classes as possible and I don't remember much about what I learned. How am I ever going to teach my kids?" Such science anxiety—with its accompanying threat of science illiteracy—is becoming frighteningly widespread. Responses to an article titled "Why We Need to Understand Science" by the late Carl Sagan included such comments as "Not one kid in this school likes science," "My child is fascinated by science, but she doesn't get any in school or on TV," and—dismally—"Why is the basketball coach teaching chemistry?"

Ours is an overwhelmingly scientific and technological age;

a thorough grounding in science is essential for making rational decisions about issues that will affect all our lives. (Should we save the spotted owl? Are irradiated foods dangerous? Should we outlaw genetic engineering? Do power lines cause cancer?) Even more important is the habit of scientific thought: a combination of open curiosity, skeptical scrutiny, and weighing of available evidence that allows us to make sense of the world, to separate fact from fable, to protect ourselves from charlatans. Do crystals have healing powers? Prove it. Design a properly controlled experiment and show me the data.

Science, of all subjects, may be the most rewarding to study: a marvelous discipline filled with fascinations, surprises, and—show me the child who can resist this—messily entrancing hands-on activities. Of all subjects, it may also be the most massive, encompassing as it does an enormous array of specialties, among them astronomy, botany, cell and molecular biology, entomology, environmental science, evolution, marine biology, mircrobiology, ornithology, physiology, zoology, geology, meteorology, paleontology, chemistry, and physics. This intimidating list does not mean that anyone needs to teach all of the above. A genuine interest in any scientific topic—plants, planets, or pterodactyls—leads inevitably to a well-rounded educational experience. Your child is interested in dinosaurs? Chances are you will visit museums, read endless books about dinosaurs, learn the ins and outs of dinosaur anatomy and taxonomy, and discover the scope of geologic time—"When *was* the Jurassic, anyway?" You may go on a fossil hunt, learn what paleontologists do, find out why fossils are found in sedimentary rock, and make a few sample fossils—try plaster of Paris—of your own. You'll build dinosaur models. You'll learn about theories of dinosaur extinction—which may lead you, willy-nilly, into studies of asteroids, Apollo objects, and craters. You'll find out what the dinosaurs ate—"How were plants different then?"—and sharpen your mathematical skills by comparing dinosaur weights, heights, and lengths. ("Which was bigger: an ultrasaurus or a blue whale?") You'll investigate theories of warm-blooded versus cold-blooded dinosaurs—"What does it mean to have cold blood?"—discover how paleontologists determine the age of their specimens, and learn about amber, DNA, and the biochemistry of cloning.

For the nervous, there are many superb science resources commercially available: informational books, activity books, videos, computer software, kits, manuals, and laboratory equipment. The Internet is a rich source of science information, demonstrations, tutorials, and museum tours. Best for beginners: determine what interests your kids. Do they like bugs, chemistry sets, stargazing, gardening? Then find a couple of hands-on activity books—try your local library or bookstore—and fool around. An awful lot of scientists got their start in the backyard, catching crickets, or in the kitchen, combining baking soda and vinegar and—round-eyed—watching them bubble and fizz.

Science Resources

The Best of Wonderscience: Elementary Science Activities.

Kessler, James; Delmar, 1997.
Over 400 science activities for kids in grades 4–6, with thorough background explanations, instructions, and color illustrations. The experiments were chosen to fulfill the National Science Education Standards (see below).

Free Stuff for Science Buffs.

Young, Barry; Coriolis Group Books, 1996.
Interesting information and lots of free stuff—much of it on-line—for young scientists.

Great Explorations in Math and Science (GEMS) Series

An excellent series of activity books/teachers' manuals on a wide range of scientific topics from the Lawrence Hall of Science.
University of California
ATTN LHS Store
Lawrence Hall of Science, #5200
Berkeley, CA 94720-5200
(510) 642-7771
e-mail: GEMS@uclink.berkeley.edu
Web site: www.lhs.berkeley.edu

Making and Using Scientific Equipment.

Newton, David E.; Franklin Watts, 1993.
Complete instructions for building many scientific instruments for your home laboratory.

National Science Education Standards.
National Committee on Science Education Standards and Assessment; National Academy Press, 1996.
What kids are expected to know in science from grades K–12. The text of the book is also available on-line at www.nap.edu/readin groom/books/nses.

Science Through Children's Literature.
Butzow, Carol M., and John W. Butzow; Teacher Ideas Press, 1988.
Science activities and experiments linked to 30 popular picture books for kids in grades K–3. Also see *More Science Through Children's Literature* (Teacher Ideas Press, 1998).

SCIENCE CATALOGS

American Science & Surplus
3605 Howard St.
Skokie, IL 60076
(847) 982-0870
Web site: www.sciplus.com

Aves Science Kits
Box 229
Peru, ME 04290

Carolina Biological Supply Co.
2700 York Rd.
Burlington, NC 27215
(800) 334-5551
Web site: www.carolina.com

Delta Hands-On Science
Box 3000
Nashua, NH 03061-3000
(800) 442-5444
Web site: www.delta-ed.com

Edmund Scientific Co.
620 Lakeview Pkwy.
Vernon Hills, IL 60061
(800) 445-5985
Web site: www.edsci.com

Scientific Explorer, Inc.
2802 E. Madison
Suite 114
Seattle, WA 98112
(206) 322-7611 or
(800) 900-1182
Web site:
www.scientificexplorer.com

TOPS Learning Systems
10970 S. Mulino Rd.
Canby, OR 97013
Web site: www.topscience.com

Wild Goose Co.
375 Whitney Ave.
Salt Lake City, UT 84115
(801) 466-1172 or
(800) 373-1498

HISTORY/GEOGRAPHY

How should history be taught? Traditionally the schools have taken an "expanding horizons" approach to the social studies, in which children begin close to home, studying themselves, and then expand their knowledge in ever-widening circles to studies of families, neighborhoods, and towns, then state, country, and world. As the social face of America has changed, however, the traditional approach to history has become less relevant to students' everyday lives. Even the definition of *family*—so straightforward in the 1950s—is now subject to debate. The majority of school-age children today live in single-parent homes—and what about kids who live with grandparents, in foster homes, or with two mothers or two fathers? In studies of families, shouldn't such groups get equal time?

Social conflicts have always been fought on the well-trampled ground of the public-school history curriculum, under the assumption that what we teach our children about the past determines their views of the present and future. What about the contribution of minority groups to history? What about feminist history? Multicultural history? What about history from the point of view of the American Indians? Was Columbus really a hero? How about that debt-ridden slaveholder Thomas Jefferson? Those who support such a purpose for history studies, however, miss the point. History should not be used to inculcate a specific government-approved social agenda. History, like science, should be presented as an ongoing journey of discovery, a continual reappraisal and reassessment of facts in a search for understanding and truth. Was Columbus a hero? Yes. A villain? Yes again. History is complex; and to the real questions, there are no simple answers. If our kids learn that, they've learned an essential lesson.

At the heart of history, however—with all its conflicts, questions, interpretations, and debates—are stories. "History is stories," writes Joy Hakim, author of the superb American history series *A History of US*, "true stories—the best ever." These stories may be the surest route to a fascination with history: tales of knights and castles, Greek myths, multicultural folktales, Indian legends, adventure stories.

History/Geography Resources

Geography for Life.
National Geographic Society.
Detailed curriculum guidelines for the national geography standards for grades K–12, illustrated with photographs, maps, and diagrams.
National Geographic Society
Box 1640
Washington, DC 20013-1640
(800) 368-2728

Historical Literacy: The Case for History in American Education.
Gagnon, Paul, and the Bradley Commission on History in Schools, eds.; Houghton Mifflin, 1989.
A convincing argument for the central position of history in education, with detailed descriptions of the various ways in which history programs can be organized.

A History of U.S. Series.
Hakim, Joy; Oxford University Press.
A 10-volume American history series for kids aged 8–13. Each illustrated book is 150 to 200 pages long; all are well researched, informational, and thoroughly absorbing.

It Happened in America.
Perl, Lila; Henry Holt, 1996.
Read your way across America with 51 delightful (and true) stories, one from each of the fifty states, plus one (starring Dolley Madison) from the District of Columbia.

Kids' America.
Caney, Steven; Workman, 1978.
Adventures in hands-on American history from colonial days to the 20th century. The book is packed with information, activities, projects, puzzles, recipes, and games.

Social Studies Through Children's Literature: An Integrated Approach.
Fredericks, Anthony D.; Teacher Ideas Press, 1991.
History through 32 popular children's picture books. For each is included a plot summary, a list of discussion questions, and many related projects and activities.

History/Geography Catalogs

Bluestocking Press
Box 2030
Shingle Springs, CA 95682-2030
(916) 622-8586 or
(800) 959-8586

Social Studies School Service
History, World History, and Geography Catalogs
10200 Jefferson Blvd.
Box 802
Culver City, CA 90232-0802
(310) 839-2436 or
(800) 421-4246
Web site: socialstudies.com

FOREIGN LANGUAGES

Kids under 12 learn languages best. It's an unfair glitch in human brain wiring: our language window, so receptively open in toddlerhood, slams shut by puberty. We can, of course, learn languages as adolescents and adults, but it's more difficult and—by the teen years—we've lost all hope of ever mastering such pronunciation challenges as the notorious French *r*. The earlier you start, the better.

If you're lucky enough to be bilingual, speak both languages to your kids.

There are many foreign-language programs available for kids of all ages, in audio, video, and computer software versions, all of which allow young users to listen and repeat, in more or less the manner in which language is acquired in the first place. Many programs targeted at preschoolers and early elementary aged children include song tapes, which are fun and especially easy to learn, since melody and rhythm are such effective memory aids.

FOREIGN LANGUAGE RESOURCE

How to Learn a Foreign Language.
Charles, Arthur H.; Franklin Watts, 1994.
Useful suggestions for approaching foreign language studies, targeted at kids aged 12 and up.

FOREIGN LANGUAGE CATALOGS

American Classical League
Miami University
Oxford, OH 45056
(513) 529-7741

Audio-Forum
96 Broad St.
Guilford, CT 06437
(203) 453-9794 or (800) 243-1234

National Textbook Company
Foreign Languages Catalog
4255 W. Touhy Ave.
Lincolnwood, IL 60646-1975
(708) 679-5500 or
(800) 323-4900

Penton Overseas, Inc.
2470 Impala Dr.
Carlsbad, CA 92008
(619) 431-0060 or (800) 748-5804
Web site: www.pentonoverseas.com

Teach Me Tapes
B-1 Opus Center, Suite 100
9900 Bren Rd. E.
Minnetonka, MN 55343-9664
(800) 456-4656

ART/MUSIC

Art and music are easy to incorporate into daily homeschool life. Kids, supplied with materials, will happily draw, paint, model with clay, construct wood-scrap sculptures, experiment with mosaics, or try their hands at a laptop loom—or will equally happily listen to Bach at bedtime, dance around the living room to the strains of *The Nutcracker Suite,* or thrill to the musical tale of *Peter and the Wolf.* Most communities provide art, crafts, and music classes for kids and families. Homeschoolers, asked about their children's social life, often cite extracurricular art and music classes.

ART/MUSIC RESOURCES

Art From Many Hands.
Schuman, Jo Miles; Davis Publications, 1984.
An excellent collection of creative multicultural art projects for kids aged 5 and up, categorized by geographical region.

The Complete Idiot's Guide to Classical Music.
Sherman, Robert, and Philip Seldon; Alpha Books, 1997.
Over 300 reader-friendly pages of information and suggestions for families of classical novices.

Drawing on the Right Side of the Brain.
Edwards, Betty; J. P. Tarcher, 1989.
A drawing course for the artistically challenged, which emphasizes the use of spatial skills localized on the right side of the brain. Too many of us, explains Edwards, attempt to draw using left-brain-centered memories, rather than reproducing what we actually see.

Drawing With Children.
Brookes, Mona; Putnam Publishing Group, 1996.
A complete art program for children aged 4 and up, in which drawing skills are taught through an "alphabet" of basic shapes. By the same author, also see **Drawing With Older Children and Teens** (J. P. Tarcher, 1991).

Encouraging the Artist in Your Child (Even If You Can't Draw).
Warner, Sally; St. Martin's Press, 1989.
"Failure-proof" art projects for kids aged 2–10.

Glues, Brews, and Goos: Recipes and Formulas for Almost Any Classroom Project.
Marks, Diana F.; Teacher Ideas Press, 1996.
Recipes for everything from paint and paper to bubble soap.

Make Mine Music!
Walther, Tom; Little, Brown, 1981.
Science, history, and hands-on projects for kids aged 8–12.

Art/Music Catalogs

Educational Record Center
3233 Burnt Mill Dr.
Suite 100
Wilmington, NC 28403
(800) 438-1637
fax (888) 438-1637
e-mail: erc-inc@worldnet.att.net
Web site: www.erc-inc.com

Far Out Explorations
Box 308
Milford, CT 06460

(203) 877-2962 or
(800) 510-ARTS

KidsArt
Box 274
Mt. Shasta, CA 96067
(530) 926-5076
fax (530) 926-5076
e-mail: kidsart@macshasta.com
Web site: www.kidsart.com

Music for Little People
Box 1460
Redway, CA 95560-1460
(800) 346-4445
fax (707) 923-3241
e-mail:
musicforlittlepeople@mflp.com
Web site: www.mflp.com

R. B. Walter Art and Craft Materials
Box 6231
Arlington, TX 76005
(800) 447-8787

S&S Arts and Crafts
Box 513
Colchester, CT 06415-0513
(800) 243-9232
fax (800) 566-6678
e-mail: service@snswwide.com
Web site: www.snswwide.com

Sax Arts and Crafts
Box 510710
New Berlin, WI 53151
(800) 558-6696 or
(800) 522-4278

West Music
Box 5521
1212 5th St.
Coralille, IA 52241
(800) 397-9378
e-mail: service@westmusic.com
Web site: www.westmusic.com

PHYSICAL EDUCATION

When homeschoolers tangle with the public schools, chances are it's not over chemistry, English literature, or Spanish, but sports. Many schools are reluctant to allow homeschoolers to compete for or occupy slots on their sports teams. While some families do manage to negotiate athletic arrangements with school officials, in general, this means that homeschooled kids hooked on basketball, football, hockey, or soccer must look elsewhere for team participation. Try a local Y.M.C.A., recreational center, or health club: many sponsor nonschool-affiliated teams.

Many homeschooled kids circumvent this problem by choosing sports that do not require coaches, playing fields, and large numbers of like-minded peers. They may swim, ski, skate, or play racquetball or tennis, jog, hike, or bicycle. Many health clubs offer gymnastics or aerobic exercise programs to groups of different ages. Or—it's the dead of winter and you don't want to leave the house—there are exercise programs for both children and adults available on video.

PHYSICAL EDUCATION RESOURCES

Everybody's a Winner: A Kid's Guide to New Sports and Fitness.
Schneider, Tom; Little, Brown, 1976.
All about sports and fitness, plus activities, projects, and do-it-yourself sports equipment and games, for kids aged 9–13.

Home School Family Fitness: A Practical Curriculum Guide.
Whitney, Bruce; Home School Family Fitness Institute, 1995.

A complete physical fitness program for kids aged 4–18, including information, instructions, lesson plans, record charts, and games.
Home School Family Fitness Institute
159 Oakwood Dr.
New Brighton, MN 55112
(612) 636-7738

Hooked On Fitness!
Harrison, James C.; Parker Publishing Company, 1993.
Many many games of all kinds for promoting physical fitness.

PHYSICAL EDUCATION CATALOGS

Collage Video
5390 Main St. NE
Minneapolis, MN 55421-1128
(800) 433-6769

The Training Camp
Genesis Direct, Inc.
100 Plaza Dr.
Secaucus, NJ 07094-3613
(800) ATHLETE

The Amateur Athletic Union (AAU) is the largest volunteer multisport organization in the United States dedicated to the support of amateur sports and physical fitness. The AAU sponsors sports programs of all kinds for kids of all ages on the local, regional, and national level. For information on an AAU branch in your area, contact:

AAU
c/o Walt Disney World Resort
Box 10,000
Lake Buena Vista, FL 32830-1000
(407) 934-7200 or (407) 363-6170

MORE TOOLS: GENERAL RESOURCE CATALOGS

The Education Connection
Box 1417
Tehachapi, CA 93581
(800) 863-3828
Web site: www.education
connection.com

Educational Insights
16941 Keegan Ave.
Carson, CA 90746
(310) 884-2000 or
(800) 933-3277
Web site: edin.com

The Home School
104 S. West Ave.
Arlington, WA 98223
(360) 435-0376 or
(800) 788-1221
Web site: www.thehomeschool.com

John Holt's Book and Music Store
2380 Massachusetts Ave.
Suite 104
Cambridge, MA 02140-1226
(617) 864-3100
Web site: www.holtgws.com

Michael Olaf's Essential Montessori
Box 1162
Arcata, CA 95521
(707) 826-1557
Web site: lama.kcc.hawaii.edu/
~soma/montessori.html

The Sycamore Tree
2179 Meyer Pl.
Costa Mesa, CA 92627
(714) 642-6750 or (800) 779-6750
Web site: www.sycamoretree.com

Zephyr Press
3316 N. Chapel Ave.
Box 66006
Tucson, AZ 85728-6006
(520) 322-5090
Web site: www.zephyrpress.com

THE BOTTOM LINE, OR HOW MUCH DOES IT ALL COST?

Good words are worth much, and cost little.

GEORGE HERBERT

A man is rich in proportion to the things he can afford to let alone.

HENRY DAVID THOREAU

"Who can really afford to homeschool?" snapped one homeschooling critic, responding to an article titled "Is Homeschooling Good for America?" in the March 14–15, 1998, issue of *USA Weekend Magazine*. "Certainly not poor, working-class, or single-parent families. Homeschooling is just another division between rich and poor." Well, guess again. The vast majority of homechoolers are ordinary middle-class working people, earning—according to Brian Ray's 1997 survey of Christian homechoolers—a median annual income of $43,000. On this, they support an average of 3.3 kids—the national average is

1.8 children per family—upon whom they spend, for educational purposes, an average of $546 per kid per year. Ray's survey doesn't detail what his 1,522 families spent this $546 *on*, but he does state that 85.6 percent of survey respondents own a home computer, 68.6 percent buy newspapers, 96.3 percent subscribe to magazines, and 23.8 percent buy complete packaged curricula. Homeschoolers taken en masse, however, tend to view survey questionnaires with a cold eye, and Ray's sample—drawn from "the membership of one large nationwide home education organization"—may not be particularly representative of the homeschooling population as a whole. "I don't think you could find one other homeschooler just like me exactly," one parent writes, "or just like any one of us."

Accordingly, a 1995 survey of homeschoolers in the San Francisco Bay Area showed a somewhat different picture. The average homeschooling family, California-style, had 2.1 children and an annual income of $55,770. Of this, they spent an average of $3,197 on homeschooling, a sum which included packaged curricula (25 percent of respondents), computer software (80 percent of respondents), books and workbooks, museum memberships, field trips, and extracurricular classes. Extracurricular classes—among them music lessons, gymnastics, science workshops, karate, ballet, swimming, Spanish, poetry-writing, oil-painting, drama, pottery, singing, and soccer—comprised the lion's share of each family's total, for an annual average of $1,560.

Our homeschooling expenditures, compared to many, are high. The largest chunk of our (somewhat uncertain) total goes for music lessons and orchestra memberships. Josh studies piano; Ethan studies violin; Caleb studies both; and the violinists play in the local youth orchestra and chamber group, which charges a membership fee to cover music and practice room rental. Total: $3,600. (Ethan is teaching *himself* to play the piano, which is free, unless you count the price of the piano, which wasn't.) Skiing for all three kids—an inexpensive program through a local homeschooling group—runs an annual $120. We subscribe to several magazines—among them *Scientific American, Discover, The New Scientist, The Skeptical Inquirer, American Heritage, Archaeology Today, Book Links,* and *Time*—and we maintain two family museum memberships. About $300. The boys usually take an annual extracurricular art or crafts class: $300 more. Science and art supplies, paper (large quantities), and books probably run around $500—a wild guess—and our book bill, now that all three boys are teenagers, will doubtless increase. All the boys use some textbooks now, which are pricey: most secondary- and college-level texts run around $50 and up. Josh has started taking supplementary classes at our local community college (tuition per class: $300). Internet access runs a monthly $20. All told, once you add in field trips, concerts, workshops, and (my favorite category) miscellaneous, we probably spend about $6,000 a year home-schooling—or, all things being equal, about $2,000 per kid. This is considerably less than the average annual amount spent per pupil by the public schools—about $5,200—and even less than the average private school tuition in our area ($6,000 to $10,000), but it's not cheap. We are not homeschooling on a shoestring.

Some of these expenditures, however, though an enriching part of the boys' homeschooling experience, are costs we would incur anyway, as a family. "We don't spend any money that we wouldn't have spent even if our kids were in school," writes a couple from West Virginia. "We would make the same pur-chases and trips whether or not we were homeschooling, so we don't consider that we have *any* homeschooling costs," states a mother from Connecticut. Some homeschoolers point out that there are many "hidden" savings to be found in educating chil-dren at home—"No school wardrobes, school lunches, or day-care fees," writes one mother—but others respond that such hidden savings are more than balanced by "hidden" costs. The largest of these by far for many homeschoolers is the loss of income suffered when one parent chooses to stay at home full-time with the children. Given the current state of our economy, when many families depend on two salaries just to meet their mortgage payments, and government policy, which does nothing to encourage stay-at-home child rearers, this problem has no simple solution. It is often an advantage to consider your educational options as early as possible, such that your major lifestyle decisions are made with a single salary in mind—but this is often easier said than done. Many homeschoolers supplement their incomes by running small home-based businesses—examples include cabinetmaking, basketry, musical instrument repair, food cooperatives, and tutorial services—or working independently at home.

Still, having kids—and educating kids—undeniably costs *something* and, for families with very limited budgets, homeschooling can be challenging. Many homeschoolers in this boat, faced with the necessity of educational penny-pinching, have turned homeschooling on a shoestring into a highly creative art. "We haunt yard and garage sales," writes a homeschooler from Seattle, Washington. "We've found games and books, bundles of fabric scraps and yarn for craft projects, stacks of *National Geographic* maps, loose-leaf notebooks (25 cents apiece), a child's easel—even an encyclopedia!" "So many community activities are absolutely free," writes a mother from Ohio. "We scan the local newspaper for concerts, sports events, craft demonstrations, and lectures. Plays and performances at the public schools are often free and open to the public." (As well they should be.) "Throwaways!" writes another. "Just ask local businesses if they have any discards that you might use for art, craft, science, or building projects. We've come up with old telephones and rolls of bell wire, wooden crates and boxes, carpet scraps, old wallpaper books, lots of useful plastic containers, and a working manual typewriter. The kids love it." "We get end rolls from the local newspaper office for drawing paper," writes a West Virginia family, "and we scrounge all the time."

BEST SUGGESTIONS
FOR LIMITED BUDGETS

1. **Use the public library.** Public libraries are near-inexhaustible and cost-free sources of educational raw material. All supply a wealth of books, reference books, magazines, and newspapers; many also offer their members science and history documentaries on video, CDs and audiocassette tapes, foreign language tapes, maps, games, lecture and film series, story hours and book discussion clubs, microfilm and microfiche machines, and computer access. Most libraries also sponsor book sales—many maintain an ongoing sale or discard rack—which can be an excellent source of inexpensive books for those building their own home libraries.

2. **Make/write your own materials.** Many of our sons' favorite and most effective educational materials have been homemade. Caleb's preferred early readers were a series of small stapled paper booklets, hand-printed and -illustrated, detailing the adventures of Bad Bob the Sheep, a bug-eyed and ill-behaved animal who gluttonously ate everything in sight, including grass, trees, flowers, houses, an entire pirate ship, and—finally—the moon. (Sample line: "No, Bob, no!") The boys read them, giggled over them, colored in them, and eventually, inspired by them, began writing their own Bob stories.

The boys also made their own alphabet/phonics books, using spiral-bound notebooks from the supermarket. They printed the relevant upper- and lowercase letter at the top of each page, then illustrated each with their own drawings or with pictures cut from magazines. (These never worked out quite as expected: *A*, Josh explained patiently, was *not* for Spider—as I had so nervously assumed—but for Arachnid; and *B*, dramatically illustrated with a lightning-struck gentleman flying a kite, was for Benjamin Franklin.)

Math materials are easy to fabricate at home: plain Popsicle sticks, for example, make terrific math manipulatives; if you don't manage to save enough of your own over the long hot summer, they're sold in inexpensive packs of 100 or more as "craft sticks." Dried beans, pasta (uncooked), and M&Ms can be used for counting and sorting games. And the neighborhood five-and-dime is a handy source for homeschool math materials: most carry packets of play money, dominoes, dice, plastic rulers, and cheap but serviceable chess and checkers sets.

Invent your own creative writing or storytelling program, tailored to the interests and imaginations of your own kids. All it takes is a pack of index cards. Write a suggestion for a creative writing project on each card; have the kids pick one at random when they want a challenge or a new idea. *(In an old chest in the attic, you find an ancient map showing on island on which there is a buried treasure. What do you think the map looks like? Tell about how you get there and what you find on the island.)*

Or try making your own games. Our kids' favorite geography game was homemade, consisting of a world map *(National Geographic,* library book sale, 50 cents) and another pack of those handy index cards, each with a geography question. The boys would take turns identifying sites on the map: "Where would you go to see the world's highest waterfall?" "Where would you go to find penguins?" "Find the country where Robin Hood lived." "An asteroid is going to splash down in the Pacific Ocean tomorrow. Where do you think we should go? Why?" "Where did Paddington Bear come from?"

The boys also collaborated on a series of homemade board games, usually drawn on posterboard using felt-tipped marking pens, with playing pieces made from cardboard or oven-baked clay. Game topics have included imaginative adventure and fantasy games, planet-hopping through the solar system, sailing around the world with Magellan (who, in our version, occasionally survives his ill-fated encounter in the Philippines, only to get eaten by a sea monster), traveling to Cathay with Marco Polo, hiking to the Pacific with Lewis and Clark (a truly daunting board, with squares labeled Trap, Dangerous Cliffs, and Eaten by Bear), and escaping north to Canada on the Underground Railroad. Game-making can be as much of a learning experience as game-playing. Designing a good game may involve background reading, research, and lots of questions and discussion—and it costs next to nothing. And it's fun.

3. **Ask about family and educators' discounts.** As home-schoolers, you're doubtless eligible for one or the other of these (or both), which may add up to substantial savings. A family museum membership, for example, often pays for itself quickly: most allow unlimited visits and discounts at museum-sponsored workshops and classes.

4. **Read catalogs and reviews.** First, if you have limited funds, make sure that when you do fork over the money for something it's exactly what you want. Is it versatile enough to last through several children? Is it a consumable resource—which means that one child uses it up and that's it? Does it have prolonged interest potential or is it a one-shot deal, such that the kids will quickly become bored?

Second, know what's out there. The natural inclination, during belt-tightening budgetary periods, is to avoid all sources of temptation. Educational resource catalogs, however, are more than collections of upsettingly unaffordable stuff: they are excellent sources of home-adaptable ideas. Survey the selections. Versions of many games, manipulatives, and activity books can be devised with ordinary materials at home—none as glitzy as the commercial models, perhaps, but the homemade versions can be personalized, tailored to fit your children's needs precisely.

5. **Remember that learning happens everywhere.** Many superb learning experiences occur on a walk in the woods or a stroll in the park, during an afternoon spent puttering in the

kitchen or an evening spent on the rug in front of the wood-stove. William Wimsatt, college dropout and inspired self-educator, described his plans for his personal curriculum in a recent issue of the *Utne Reader:* all centered around the rich conglomeration of learning experiences inherent in daily life. Wimsatt, for example, planned to get to know someone new every day—a volunteer, a community worker, a craftsperson, a lecturer; to attend a different place of worship every Sunday; to read voraciously; and to devise his own personal Bible, almanac, and telephone directory.

Worlds can be found by a child and an adult bending down and looking together under the grass stems or at the skittering crabs in a tidal pool.

MARY CATHERINE BATESON

"Money can't buy you happiness," my grandfather used to say. "But," he always added regretfully, "it sure can be useful." Similarly, money—despite its obvious usefulness in obtaining such items as microscopes, geometry textbooks, and new violin strings—is not the secret to a good education. Learning, ultimately, is a personal act, fostered in an atmosphere of trust, support, and love. Time spent with our children costs us nothing and is worth the earth. That's what parents have going for them.

One father is more than 100 schoolmasters.

GEORGE HERBERT

RESOURCES

BOOKS

Cut Your Spending in Half Without Settling for Less: How to Pay the Lowest Price for Everything.
Editors of Rodale Press; Rodale Press, 1995.
Valuable how-tos for the financially strapped.

Free and Almost Free Things for Teachers.
Osborn, Susan; Perigee Books, 1993.
A lot of creative and educational stuff, all free or very, very cheap.

Gobs and Gobs of Free Stuff.
Lesko, Matthew; Information USA, 1995.
Lots of interesting free stuff, much of it informational and educational, plus directory of state information.
Information USA, Inc.
Box E
Kensington, MD 20895
(301) 924-0556 or
(800) UNCLE SAM
Web site: www.lesko.com

A Kid's Guide to Finding Good Stuff.
Klein, Bill; Harbinger House, 1994.
A manual for scroungers aged 8 and up, with proper cautions on safety, permissions, and respect for private and public properties.

RESOURCES FOR PENNY-PINCHERS

One Income Living in a Two Income World
Web site: members.aol.com/DSimple/index.html
Filled with creative ideas for living simply by a homeschooling mother of three.

Back Home Magazine
Box 70
Hendersonville, NC 28793
(800) 992-2546
e-mail: backhome@ioa.com
Web site:
www.ioa.com/home/backhome/
A magazine dedicated to an independent lifestyle, with articles on home businesses, homeschooling, do-it-yourself building projects, and gardening.
6 issues/$18.97

The Dollar Stretcher Newsletter
Box 23785
Fort Lauderdale, FL 33307
A multifaceted guide to saving money.
12 issues/$18

Free Materials for Schools and Libraries
Connaught Education Services
Box 34069
Dept. 349
Seattle, WA 98124
A newsletter of freebies; each 16-page issue contains 80 to 100 new items.
5 issues/$17

The Homeschool Exchange

Box 1378
Boerne, TX 78006-1378
(210) 336-2021
fax (210) 336-3105
e-mail: hsxchange@aol.com

A buy-sell-trade newspaper for home educators. Items, all at substantial savings, are listed by academic subject.

6 issues/$6.50

Homeschooling on a Shoestring

Web site:
www.geocities.com/Athens/4663/

Money-saving tips, freebies, recipes, on-line resources, downloadable unit studies, and regional support group lists for the financially strapped.

Homeschooler's Used Curriculum Sites

Web site: www.geocities.com/
Athens/8259/used.html

A long list of sites where homeschoolers can buy and sell used educational materials on line.

The Penny Pincher

Box 809
Kings Park, NY 11754

Helpful tips and creative tips from a homeschooling mother of four.

Sample issue/$1 plus SASE
12 issues/$15

The Tightwad Gazette

Box 3570
Leeds, ME 04263-9710

Creative savings ideas for families.

Sample issue/SASE
12 issues/$12

BEYOND THE
HOME

Home is not where you live but where they understand
you.

CHRISTIAN MORGENSTERN

Many opponents of homeschooling focus their criticisms on
the academic qualifications of the teaching parents. Home-
based learning is severely handicapped, the argument goes,
because it is conducted under the auspices of parents who cannot possibly be proficient in the many academic subjects
required for a well-rounded education. Parents are amateurs,
vainly striving to fill the large-size shoes of professional experts.
"Teachers are trained professionals with an abundance of
expertise to offer," writes sixth-grade teacher Tracy Pope in the
August 1997 issue of *Bay Area Parent*. "Kids belong in our classrooms. To repair your car, would you take it to a dentist?"

In a sense, there is some validity to this criticism. The truth
of the matter is that—in all likelihood—neither parents *nor*
teachers are adequately proficient in all academic subjects to be
all things to all students. A common homeschool question concerns the teaching of what are commonly assumed to be the

"hard" subjects: "How will you deal with algebra? Chemistry? Calculus?" As I've said before, such defined secondary-level subjects are a piece of cake in comparison to the challenging questions asked every five minutes by a curious six-year-old. "How does a laser work?" "How hot is the center of the sun?" "What's inside a camel's hump?" "How do dolphins talk? Do they have a voice box?" "What keeps the worker bees from eating royal jelly?" Few of us are so well prepared in electronics, physics, zoology, and entomology that we can readily reel off the answers to all (any?) of the above—and none of us should be expected to. The ideal teacher is not an Olympian font of knowledge but a facilitator, a supportive helper in a student's quest for enlightenment. You don't know the answers? Sure you do. They are: "Let's look it up." "Why don't we go to the library?" "We've got a videotape all about dolphins—want to watch it?" "Let's see if there's a beekeeper in the phone directory—maybe he or she can tell us." "How about the Internet?"

The idea that all learning must be dished out to us by experts is a second misconception. The public schools, states John Taylor Gatto, foster intellectual dependency: the message they disseminate is "Good students wait to be told what to do." No teacher should perpetuate a mind-set of mental helplessness; a good teacher empowers. I remember our youngest son's first piano lesson, a little over a year ago. Caleb had taught himself to play the piano—by ear, with the help of a do-it-yourself book—but he needed help to progress. The session started poorly. The teacher—a pleasant man who had cats, kites, and a flower garden—was a demanding instructor; Caleb—I was eavesdropping from the kitchen—was beginning to answer him in resentful monosyllables. Impasse, I thought dismally, and worriedly began to wonder about what to do next. The teacher clearly felt the same. There was an awful pause. Then, in an instant, all turned around. "Look," the teacher said to Caleb, "you're taking these lessons so that you'll be able to do this on your own. When we're through, you'll be able to take a piece of music—any piece of music—and you'll know how to analyze it so that you can tackle it by yourself. I can't make you a pianist, but I can help you start. See this…" Caleb saw. This was what he wanted. A fellow musician was giving him a tool.

Caleb's piano teacher is a case in point: sooner or later most parents find some subject area in which their kids need or want more than they have to offer. Sometimes you do need a knowledgeable expert. A kid bent on studying physics, for example, benefits from a teacher who knows his or her physics; and—unless your French accent is straight off the streets of Paris—your kids may learn their French *r*'s better from someone who can pronounce them. "Homeschooling" doesn't mean an education obtained solely behind one's own front door. There are a number of false images of homeschooling, writes Vermont homeschooler Cindy Wade. "First of all, many of us don't *school*, and secondly, we don't stay at *home* to learn. Home is only our base, from where we branch out in all directions, including the backyard, the community, the country, and the world at large."

Most young homeschoolers' first forays into the outer world are through participation in field trips. Field trips are an integral part of most homeschool programs, providing mind-broadening enrichment, opportunities for active hands-on learning, and a chance to interact with a wide range of people with an equally wide range of interests. When our kids were younger, one day a week was always reserved for field trips—which encompassed anything from a nature hike in the woods behind the house to a full-fledged all-day expedition to the art museum. My sole rule of thumb when it comes to field trips: keep it small. There are some advantages inherent in being part of a large group—discounted entrance fees, for example—but none outweigh the benefits of the small. Single-family field trips are ideal: these give your kids the chance to focus on the experience at hand, rather than the social distractions of the group. The small atmosphere encourages relaxed talk, exchange of questions and answers, thoughtful observations. This doesn't mean that small field trips are solemnly intellectual affairs—they're fun, but they're also fruitful. For contrast, take a look at the average school group touring a science center or historical site: children yelling, tussling, unable to make their questions heard—if they have any—made to dawdle over exhibits that don't interest them, rushed through exhibits that do. The guide/teacher has an impossible task; there is no way to provide thirty restless nine-year-olds with wildly different interests the sort of individual attention they need.

A homeschooling friend from Arizona writes: "This Tuesday we went on a field trip to the Peanut Patch, where peanuts are grown, harvested, and processed into delightful butters and confections. The children were given a first-rate tour, which included the history of peanuts in America, an explanation of how peanuts grow, and the story of how the owner of the Peanut Patch came to own the land, grow peanuts, and establish his business there. Then they tromped through the fields and were allowed to pull up peanut bushes to see the goobers clinging to the roots, and were shown (and allowed to poke around) various planting and harvesting machines, which were standing idle because the harvest has been delayed this year. We saw the peanut storage shed, walked through the sorting and shelling areas, and ended up in the kitchens, where workers were busy making candies. Finally we went to the peanut store, where the children used the peanut-butter machine to grind peanuts into fresh unadulterated peanut butter. We took it home, along with a couple of bags of nuts."

Another describes a trip to a craftsperson's workshop: "An acquaintance allowed us to visit her workshop, where she does stained-glass crafts. She helped the boys draw designs (sail-boats) on paper, then cut patterns, select and cut the glass, and solder the pieces together with lead and copper. The boys now each have a finished sun catcher hanging in the bedroom window. It was an ususual experience for them, since they'd never seen stained-glass work before…"

From my homeschool journal:

◆ **March 12, 1991**

We went to the Old North Bridge in Concord [Massachusetts] today, where we figured out where the Americans and British were positioned when the fighting began, discussed Emerson's poem ("Concord Hymn"), and admired the statue of the Minuteman. Then visited the Concord Antiquarian Museum where we saw Paul Revere's lantern, Emerson's study, an assortment of Thoreau memorabilia, and miscellaneous colonial items. Not a great museum—it's small, and not much on labeling—but the kids found plenty to interest them. "Look at that strange little chair that just fits in a corner!" "What kind of piano is this?" "Who was Thoreau?" "What was Walden? *Could kids read it?" "Is Walden Pond near here? Can we go see it?" "I know who Emerson was—he wrote that poem about 'the shot heard round the world'!" "How old was the kid who made this sampler?" And so on and on. I love going to museums with the boys. A museum docent—attracted by all the questions—came over and talked with them for a long time and told them several stories about nineteenth-century residents of Concord, including Louisa May Alcott. Josh now plans to read* Little Women *and* Little Men.

Homeschoolers have the freedom and flexibility to build an education from a multiplicity of sources. Often they tap into the collective expertise of the community, seeking out tutors, mentors, advisers, supplementary classes, courses, and workshops. Solutions for teaching the "hard" subjects, depending on what you're looking for—tatting instructions? history tutorials? bassoon lessons?—are varied. Perhaps the most obvious these days is electronic: the home computer.

The computer, for many of us, has changed the face of homeschooling, providing ready access to the world beyond—

far beyond—the home. Computers—via the Internet and the World Wide Web—open doors to a mind-boggling store of information and provide the option, through creative software, for a wide range of interactive educational activities. (Among these is blowing up animated enemy spaceships, an activity that—my children assure me—is essential for the development of adequate hand-eye coordination.) Computer users can take virtual tours of museums, art galleries, and historical sites; explore the planets of the solar system; view electron micrographs of viruses; listen to recordings of famous speeches; track down maps, biographies, literary texts, dictionaries, encyclopedias, quotation collections, timelines, mathematical puzzles, and games. They can participate in chat room sessions; take online tutorials, workshops, and classes; find pen pals; publish their poems and short stories; ask questions of scientists; get help with their geometry homework. A young Shakespeare enthusiast, for example, can access the complete text of *Hamlet*, track down a biography of Shakespeare, explore the Globe Theatre, learn about everyday life in Elizabethan England, view film clips of modern Shakespearean performances, and call up a timeline of Shakespeare's plays. "Computers make do-it-yourself education downright efficient," writes homeschooling proponent David Churbuck. "Your child can probably learn spelling or arithmetic or a foreign language faster on a computer than in a crowded classroom."

COMPUTER RESOURCES

Children and the Internet: A Zen Guide for Parents and Educators.
Kehoe, Brendan and Victoria Mixon; Prentice Hall, 1997.
How to integrate the Internet into educational programs, with detailed lists of on-line educational resources.

Children's Software Revue
A bimonthly magazine of reviews of software programs and Web sites for kids aged 2–15.
    6 issues/$24
Children's Software Revue
44 Main St.
Flemington, NJ 08822
(800) 993-9499
fax (908) 284-0405
Web site: www.childrenssoftware.com

Internet Family Fun: The Parent's Guide to Safe Surfing.
Bruno, Bonnie, with Joel Comm; no starch press, 1997.
How to navigate the Net ("without a bunch of technical mumbo jumbo"), plus reviews of 250 interesting Web sites for kids.

The Internet Kids and Family Yellow Pages.
Armour, Polly Jean; Osborne/McGraw-Hill, 1997.
Descriptions of over 3,000 interesting, educational, and "kid-safe" listings selected by a children's librarian.

LearningWare Reviews
A monthly on-line magazine of educational software reviews, available to subscribers by e-mail.
  12 issues/$5.95
LearningWareReviews
1447 E. Country Lane
Tooele, UT 84074
fax (801) 269-0656
Web site: members.aol.com/juline/

Virtual Field Trips.
Cooper, Gail, and Garry Cooper; Teacher Ideas Press, 1997.
Internet "field trips" for kids in preschool through grade 12, grouped by academic subject.

There's more to life, however, than the world on-screen. Many experiences simply cannot be gained electronically, no matter how much global enrichment is available at the click of a button. Hands-on real-world encounters also have their educational place: on-line sources, for example, may tell you a great deal about the anatomy, physiology, taxonomy, and evolution of horses, but can't substitute for a day on the trail in the saddle; Internet research may turn up a history of Chinese ceramics, photographs of Grecian urns, a treatise on Navajo coiled pots, an explanation of the workings of a pottery kiln, and a list of recipes for glazes, but can't match the messy experience of producing your very own pot (even if it's slightly lopsided) on a potter's wheel.

"John (10) spent two days last week working for our local vet," writes a homeschooler from Virginia, "and he's even more determined to go into veterinary medicine. He participated in every aspect of the veterinary business: fed animals, cleaned cages, helped hold animals during examinations, gave pills, took temperatures, weighed animals—he even went along on a house call, to check on a sick pony. He's hoping, when he's a little older, that this could work into a full-time job…" "An elderly neighbor is teaching the girls to knit," writes a mother from New York. Our sons, all enthusiastic beginning potters, have adopted a mentor from the local arts center: their former pottery teacher, now a friend and adviser willing to provide help, hints, and encouragement.

The kids want to study Japanese, ornithology, or physics, and you feel you can't cope. One possibility is to track down a tutor.

1. **Ask.** Canvas friends, family, other homeschoolers. Many experienced homeschoolers have built up extensive social networks and may be able to direct you toward a possible coach: a foreign exchange student, a retired professional, a kid-friendly hobbyist.

2. **Exchange.** Homeschool support groups and local communities are filled with persons of many skills and talents. Often families seeking help in one field can negotiate an educational trade: recorder lessons for Spanish sessions, for example; art projects for chemistry coaching.

3. **Advertise.** Pin a notice to the public library bulletin board or take out an ad in the local paper asking for a tutor. State your kids' ages and your proposed pay rate. (If negotiable, say so.) Often college students, retirees, and others are interested in part-time employment.

4. **Recruit.** If you have specific academic needs—a math or Spanish tutor, for example—try calling the relevant department of a local college to ask if there are any students interested in part-time tutoring. Contact members of the professional community. A friendly instrument maker, weaver, gardener, or woodworker may be willing to allow visits or even take on a young apprentice.

Homeschoolers not only learn from the community, they are often heavily involved in it. Many homeschooled kids move beyond the home into community service projects or volunteer programs. Possibilities for young volunteers include libraries, museums, nursing homes, animal shelters, community service groups, art centers, and businesses. Sometimes the public schools welcome homeschooled volunteers—our kids helped set up a fifth-grade chess program. Many organizations have formal volunteer programs: these sometimes have specific volunteer requirements, including age limits. If your kids are determined, you can often negotiate a compromise by volunteering as a family group: go, and take the kids with you.

◆ January 3, 1991

Today was Josh's first day as a library volunteer. He's the library's youngest volunteer (nine) and the only children's room volunteer; he negotiated the arrangement himself last month by talking to the new children's librarian. He is simply delighted; today was too excited to eat lunch. He spent two hours at the library, putting cards in alphabetical order in the card catalog, learning to shelve books, and designing an enormous story-hour poster (a dragon), to be hung in the library doorway. The librarian wants him to write and illustrate a "big book" for her to read to the story-hour kids, and gave him a sheaf of giant-size paper to take home. Josh, ecstatic, is planning a story about a giant teddy bear.

Books

Community Service-Learning: A Guide to Including Service in the Public School Curriculum.
Wade, Rahima C., ed.; State University of New York Press, 1997.

The Kid's Guide to Service Projects.
Lewis, Barbara A.; Free Spirit Publishing, 1996.

HOMESCHOOLED TEENAGERS: ON TO COLLEGE?

Don't be afraid to take a big step if one is indicated. You can't cross a chasm in two small jumps.

DAVID LLOYD GEORGE

Whatever you can do,
Or dream you can do,
Begin it.

GOETHE

A cruel lesson of parenthood is that babies, inevitably and rapidly, grow up. Toddlerhood, when one is immersed in it, seems likely to go on forever, in an endless daily round of juice, applesauce, blocks, picture books, and footed pajamas. Almost before you know it, however, their feet are bigger than yours are, they can reach the top shelf of the kitchen cupboards (without so much as standing on tiptoe), and they're ready for high school. Ten years ago, the homeschool population was what one observer called an "entry-level market": the vast majority of homeschooled kids were under ten. Now this crew has grown up, and they—combined with the huge influx of new homeschoolers—have generated a shift in demographics. At least a third of today's homeschooled students, according to one estimate, are teenagers.

In my experience, as homeschooled kids grow older they become more and more opinionated about the content and course of their own educations. (Whose education is it, anyway?) There's an old and cautionary saying: "Be careful what you wish for, because you may get it." This neatly sums up life with the homeschooled adolescent. Randy and I chose to teach our kids at home because we wanted independent thinkers. We got them. Thus our ongoing family debate over the importance of general education credits. "I—am—doing—this," says Joshua in patient tones, looking up from his textbook, "but I can tell you that I will never in my future life *need* to do algebra." "I'll bet if you lined up all the physicists in America," says Ethan ominously, "you wouldn't find one of them who would tell a future physicist that he *needs* to read Shakespeare." "Everything that has happened since the Crusades is boring," says Caleb.

They're all right, of course. An education is a unique personal construct, powered by individual interests and needs. How many of us—other than physicists and mechanics—remember how to calculate torque? How many of us, despite all those high school French lessons, speak the language fluently? How many of us, other than Chinese scholars and history buffs, can produce any pertinent information about the Ming Dynasty? This is the root dilemma of secondary-level schooling: how to decide, once students have the basic tools for extended learning, what body of facts and figures all should know? The professional choices, which result in the public school curriculum, are necessarily arbitrary. Why learn geology but not ornithology? Why study George Eliot but not Jane

Austen? Why study trigonometry at all, if one's interests lie solely in Russian history? It's these arbitrary bureaucratic choices, however, that dominate standardized tests and channel, to a large extent, college admissions.

National Standards in American Education: A Citizen's Guide.
Ravitch, Diane; Brookings Institute, 1996.
   The pros and cons of national educational standards, plus a list of the goals adopted by Congress in 1994.

Josh is sixteen. His interests are almost wholly literary; he plans to pursue a career as a writer. He probably never *will* use algebra. Chances are, for him, it's a waste of time.

But he might need it as a ticket to get into college.

College-bound kids, as well as pursuing their personal agendas, must deal with potential college admissions requirements. Most colleges expect their students to have received the equivalent of a "good" high school education, which usually constitutes nineteen to twenty-four academic credits, each equivalent to about 120 hours of academic work, in (approximately) the following fields:

English: 4 years
Mathematics: Algebra, Geometry, Trigonometry,
   Precalculus/Calculus
Science: Earth Science, Biology, Chemistry, Physics
Foreign Language: 2 years
Social Studies: 3 years (State, American, and World History,
   Geography, Civics)
Physical Education: 2 years

One possibility for home-taught secondary-level students is an accredited correspondence course culminating in a conventional high school diploma. Schools offering complete high-school programs by correspondence include:

American School
2200 E. 170th St.
Lansing, IL 60438
(708) 418-2800

Cambridge Academy
3300 SW 34th Ave.
Suite 102
Ocala, FL 34474
(800) 252-3777
fax (904) 620-0492
Web site: www.home-school.com/
Mall/Cambridge/CambridgeAcad.
html

Clonlara School Home Based Education Program
1289 Jewett St.
Ann Arbor, MI 48104
(313) 769-4515
e-mail: Clonlara@adelphi.com
Web site: www.Clonlara.org

Home Study International
12501 Old Columbia Pike
Silver Spring, MD 20914
(301) 680-6570
(800) 782-4769

ICS-Newport/Pacific High School
925 Oak St.
Scranton, PA 18515
(717) 342-7701

Keystone National High School
515 Market St.
Box 616
Bloomsburg, PA 17815
(717) 784-5220

e-mail: kschool@mail.prolog.net
Web site: www.keystone.ptd.net

Oak Meadow School
Box 740
Putney, VT 05346
(802) 387-2021
fax (802) 387-5108
e-mail: oms@oakmeadow.com
Web site: www.oakmeadow.com

Richard M. Milburn High School
14416 Jefferson Davis Hwy.
Suite 12
Woodbridge, VA 22191
(703) 494-0147

The University of Oklahoma Independent Study Department
1600 S. Jenkins
Rm. 101
Norman, OK 73072-6507
(405) 325-1921
(800) 942-5702
fax (405) 325-7687
Web site: www.occe.ou.edu/isd/

The University of Wisconsin Learning Innovations Center
605 Science Dr.
Madison, WI 63711-1074
(608) 266-9379
(888) 414-2534
fax (608) 265-9396
Web site: learn.wisconsin.edu

Also see "Independent Study and Umbrella Schools" (page 61).

Many homeschooled teens prefer to pursue their own educational programs. "The dreary rigors of education are in full swing..." writes sixteen-year-old Kendall Hailey. "The highlight of the first day was learning how little schooling Benjamin Franklin had. Inspired by my commitment to being an autodidact, I felt compelled to ask: If Benjamin Franklin had done all he had done without ever going to high school, why are we all here?" Hailey subsequently left high school a year early to educate herself—mostly by intensive reading. (Autodidact: a self-taught person.) She also wrote a book about her experiences—*The Day I Became an Autodidact*—which is an inspirational delight for any self-taught teenager (or the doubtful parent of any self-taught teenager). Along with books, try travel, suggests Grace Llewellyn, author of *The Teenage Liberation Handbook*, listing possibilities for liberated and self-educating teens. Spend time in the wilderness or on a farm. Start your own business. Become a political activist or a community volunteer. Arrange for an internship or apprenticeship. Join an archaeological dig. Write a journal. ("Don't spend all your time on mental stuff," writes Llewellyn. "It's not natural. You have your whole life to be academic.")

And what about college? Innumerable stories now attest to

The Day I Became an Autodidact.
Hailey, Kendall; Delta, 1989.

A fascinating and highly literate journal of one teenager's quest to educate herself.

The Independent Scholar's Handbook.
Gross, Ronald; Ten Speed Press, 1993.

How-tos and success stories for and about nontraditional, independent lifelong learners.

Real Lives: Eleven Teenagers Who Don't Go To School.
Llewellyn, Grace, ed.; Lowry House, 1993.

Does "teenage liberation" work? Stories of teenagers who have successfully done it.

The Teenage Liberation Handbook: How to Quit School and Get a Real Life and Education.
Llewellyn, Grace; Lowry House, 1991.

Advice and encouragement for teenagers eager to educate themselves, with creative ideas for "unschooling" in all academic subjects, approaches for tackling college without high school, and other suggestions for independent living.

---

the successful entry of homeschooled kids into colleges and universities, among them such high-powered institutions as Harvard, Vanderbilt, Cornell, Mount Holyoke, Brown, Dartmouth, and Princeton. As popularity and public acceptance of homeschooling have increased over past years, colleges have instituted admissions criteria and proceedings tailored to kids with unusual educational backgrounds. These vary from school to school; applicants should contact institutions of choice for instructions and advice. Substitutes for traditional high school transcripts include detailed narrative accounts of the home-schooling process—another excellent reason to keep a journal, portfolios of student work, summaries and accounts of any extracurricular and supplementary classes, and descriptions of "life experience" (volunteer and work experience, for example) gained in the wider community. Be prepared to make a convincing and articulate case for homeschooling and the kind of student it produces. Many colleges are interested in—even actively seeking—ususual students with backgrounds that make them stand out from the crowd. Since most homeschoolers lack conventional grades and class records, many colleges also depend heavily on letters of recommendation and those ever-recurring test scores.

Despite the cachet of individuality, homeschoolers must also prove that they can hold their own on the mainstream educational turf. College admissions are competitive—in some cases, extremely competitive, with hundreds of applicants vying for a single place in a freshman class—and much of the weeding-out among them proceeds on the basis of test scores. As tests go for would-be college students, the big guns are the Scholastic Aptitude Test (SAT) and the ACT (American College Testing Program), plus—an optional extra—the Preliminary Scholastic Aptitude Test (PSAT). Stellar scores on the PSAT—usually taken in the fall of one's junior year in high school—qualify kids for a National Merit Scholarship; it's also preliminary, which means it's a good dry run for the SAT, taken by high school seniors. The SAT (or SAT I) consists of two sections—Verbal and Math—and is intended to test general reasoning abilities rather than specific knowledge, which is why it's an "aptitude" test. Its alternative and alter ego, the ACT, includes English, math, reading comprehension, and science reasoning sections. Some homeschoolers take both; most colleges require either one or the other. Some schools also require SAT II tests, which do test specific knowledge of individual subjects and, as such, are achievement tests. There is a long list of these in all academic fields for students to choose from: subjects include English, Spanish, American history, biology, and chemistry. One note: these tests are administered only once a year, in October, and only through private or public schools. Homeschoolers must contact the appropriate school administrator to arrange to take the tests.

Some homeschoolers, depending on career goals and personal interests, choose to pursue college at home through correspondence courses, on-line classes, and/or independent study programs. An ever-growing number of colleges and universities offer on-line classes, accessible from the comfort of your computer-equipped living room, in everything from telecommunications to the history of Western civilization. Above all, advises a recent article in the *Education Life* supplement to *The New York Times* (August 2, 1998), don't rush into college prematurely. Just over 30 percent of college freshmen, according to a 1992 survey, don't return to school for their sophomore year, a figure which—given the present often-astronomical cost of college tuition—should give any of us pause. ("College is the most expensive buffet in the world—$30,000 a year—and you'd better be sure you're hungry.") Proposed alternatives sound much like the experiences that homeschooled teenagers take for granted: take a postgraduate year of high school to take classes you always wanted to but missed; try an internship or volunteer program; travel; get a job. Not every teenager wants or needs life in the academic fast lane.

I saw Harvard today. Very beautiful, but I'm afraid I was without envy for the backpack-laden students...And let us not forget that Harvard was the place Henry David Thoreau said bored him. And since he and I were born on the same day, I'm pretty sure I would have a similar reaction.

KENDALL HAILEY
THE DAY I BECAME AN AUTODIDACT

RESOURCES

College Information On-line

College Choice
www.gseis.ucla.edu/mm/cc/home.html
General information for college-bound kids, plus advice on selecting a school, completing applications, and obtaining financial aid.

The College Guide
www.jayi.com/ACG
A search function that helps kids "find the perfect college," information about the admissions process, and a sample application form to download.

Colleges That Admit Homeschoolers
www.learninfreedom.com
Questions and anwers about college admission for homeschooled kids, plus a continually updated list of colleges and universities that admit homeschoolers.

Homeschool-Teens-College
www.concentric.net/~ctcohen
Sample college application essays; lists of college admission policies; and a sample chapter of *And What About College?: How Homeschooling Leads to Admissions to the Best Colleges and Universities* by Cafi Cohen (see below).

Peterson's
www.petersons.com
Explore many educational options, including colleges and universities, study-abroad programs, summer camps, and secondary schools.

Books

"And What About College?" How Homeschooling Leads to Admissions to the Best Colleges and Universities.
Cohen, Cafi; Holt Associates, 1997.
Helpful information on preparing for and applying to college by the mother of two home-schooled college students.

Bears' Guide to Earning College Degrees Nontraditionally.
Bear, John B. and Mariah P. Bear; C&B Publishing, 1997.
Information on evaluating and applying to colleges, with a long annotated list of institutions that offer correspondence courses or other nontraditional degree programs.

But What If I Don't Want to Go to College? A Guide to Success Through Alternative Education.
Unger, Harlow G.; Checkmark Books, 1998.
A wide range of interesting alternatives for kids who want something other than conventional college.

College Connections Web Directory 1997.
Jackson, Earl Jr.; Lycos Press, 1997.
A fat paperback plus a Win/Mac CD-ROM of college and university Web sites in the United States and abroad.

College On-line: How to Take College Courses Without Leaving Home.
Duffy, James P.; John Wiley & Sons, 1997.
Lists of offerings by college or by academic subject.

From Homeschool to College and Work.
McKee, Alison; Bittersweet House.
Box 5211-H
Madison, WI 53705-5211
How to turn nontraditional studies into successful college and job applications.

The Mentor Apprentice Exchange
The Mentor Apprentice Exchange
Box 405
Canning, Nova Scotia B0P 1H0
Canada
Descriptive lists of apprenticeships in many different fields—examples include organic gardening, beekeeping, and metal sculpting—for persons of all ages in the United States and Canada.
4 issues/$22

Peterson's Guide to Four-Year Colleges.
Peterson's Guides, 1998.
Detailed information on thousands of four-year colleges nationwide, with included Win/Mac CD-ROM. Continually updated. There is a large series of Peterson's Guides, variously categorizing colleges by academic specialty or region of the country.

The Teenager's Guide to Study, Travel, and Adventure Abroad.
Council on International Educational Exchange; St. Martin's Press, 1992.
Many listings of overseas opportunities in a wide range of fields for young people.

Whole Work Catalog
The New Careers Center, Inc.
1515 23rd St.
Box 339-CT
Boulder, CO 80306
(303) 447-1087
fax (303) 447-8684
Information about different kinds of employment or ways of making a living. $1

APPENDIX: HOMESCHOOL SUPPORT GROUPS

For a list of national, international, and regional homeschool support groups, see page 88.

Alabama

Alabama Home Educators
Box 16091
Mobile, AL 36116

Alabama Home Educators Network (AHEN)
3015 Thurman Rd.
Huntsville, AL 35805
(205) 534-6401
e-mail: KaeKaeB@aol.com
Web site: members.aol.com/kaekaeb/ahen.html

Alaska

AK Homeschoolers Association
Box 230973
Anchorage, AK 99504-3527

Alaska Home Spun Educators
Box 798
Girdwood, AK 99587
e-mail: HomeSpuned@aol.com

Homeschoolers Unlimited
3790 J St., #B
Elmendorf Air Force Base, AK 99587
e-mail: Pattrsn5@aol.com

Sitka Home Education Association
506 Verstovia St.
Sitka, AK 99835
(907) 747-1483

Arizona

Apache Junction Unschoolers
Box 6341
Apache Junction, AZ 85278
e-mail: ajunschl@aol.com
Web site: members.aol.com/ajunschl

AZ Families for Home Education
Box 4661
Scottsdale, AZ 85261-4661
(800) 929-3927

SPICE
10414 W. Mulberry Dr.
Avondale, AZ 85323
(602) 877-3642
e-mail: pompey@juno.com

TELAO Home Educators
4700 N. Tonalea Trail
Tucson, AZ 85749
(520) 749-4757

Arkansas

Coalition of Arkansas Parents (CAP)
Box 192455
Little Rock, AR 72219

Home Educators of Arkansas Voicing Excellence Now (HEAVEN)
8 Glenbrook Pl.
Sherwood, AR 72120

California

Bayshore Homeschoolers
Box 13038
Long Beach, CA 90803
(562) 434-3940
e-mail: BayShorEdu@aol.com

California Hi-Desert Home Education Association
15185 Cactus St.
Hesperia, CA 92345
(619) 949-9725

California Home Education Conference
Box 231324
Sacramento, CA 95823
(916) 391-4942
e-mail: CHEC95@aol.com

California Homeschool Network (CHN)
Box 55485
Hayward, CA 94545
(800) 327-5339
e-mail: CHNMail@aol.com
Web site:
www.comenius.org/chn.htm

Central California Homeschoolers
7600 Marchant Ave.
Atascadero, CA 93422
(805) 462-0726

East Bay Family Educators
1090 Mariposa Ave.
Berkeley, CA 94707
(510) 524-1224

Home Education League of Parents (HELP)
Suite 131
3208 Cahuenga Blvd. W
Los Angeles, CA 90068

Homeschool Association of California
Box 2442
Atascadero, CA 93423
(888) 472-4440
e-mail: info@hsc.org
Web site: www.hsc.org

Homeschooling Co-op of Sacramento
15 Moses Ct.
Sacramento, CA 95823

Humboldt Homeschoolers
Box 2125
Trinidad, CA 95570
(707) 677-3290
e-mail: psmith@humboldt1.com

Los Angeles Homeschoolers
Box 1166
Malibu, CA 90265
(310) 456-5447

Marin Homeschoolers
905 Tiburon Blvd.
Tiburon, CA 94920
(415) 435-0768

Monterey Bay Christian Homeschoolers
1558 Flores St.
Seaside, CA 93955
(408) 394-9504
Web site:
www.redshift.com/~mizmooz

North Bay HomeScholars
Box 621
Vinesburg, CA 95487
(707) 939-9525
e-mail: CynMaui@metro.net

Riverside Area Home Learners
731 Mount Whitney Circle
Corona, CA 91719
(909) 279-4026

Rose Rock Homeschool Support Group of Southern California
1752 E. Avenue J
Suite 115
Lancaster, CA 93535
e-mail:
roserock@geocities.com
Web site: www.geocities.com/
Athens/Parthenon/8503/

San Diego Home Educators
210 Copley Ave.
San Diego, CA 92116
(619) 281-6581
e-mail:
lewing@sdcoe@k12.ca.us

Sierra Christian School Association
Box 2023
Portersville, CA 93257
e-mail: mishel@lightspeed.net

Sonoma County Home Schoolers Association (SCHA)
5584 Carriage Lane
Petaluma, CA 95402
(707) 765-2181

South Valley Homeschoolers Association
7500 Chestnut St.
Gilroy, CA 95020

SPICE
Box 282
Wilton, CA 95693
(916) 687-7053
e-mail: spice-sacramento@juno.com

Whittier Homeschoolers
7432 Duchess Dr.
Whittier, CA 90606

Yosemite Area Homeschoolers
Box 74
Midpines, CA 95345
(209) 742-6802

Colorado

Colorado Home Educators Association
3043 S. Laredo Circle
Aurora, CO 80013
(303) 441-9938
e-mail: chea@tmsco.com *or*
pinewood@dash.com

Colorado Home Schooling Network
1247 Harrison St.
Denver, CO 80206
(303) 369-9541

Colorado Springs Homeschool Support Group
Box 26117
Colorado Springs, CO 80936
(800) 532-7011
e-mail: board@hschool.com
Web site: www.hschool.com

The Homeschool Support Network
3110 Pony Tracks Dr.
Colorado Springs, CO 80922
(719) 596-1162
e-mail: hsncontact@aol.com

Independent Network of Creative Homeschoolers (INCH)
19062 E. Mansfield
Aurora, CO 80013
(303) 699-9130

Mesa Verde Homeschoolers
Box 134
Mancas, CO 81328
(970) 892-7802

Rocky Mountain Education Connection
20774 E. Buchanan Dr.
Aurora, CO 80011
(303) 341-2242
e-mail: connect@pcisys.net

Secular Homeschool Support Group
Colorado Springs, CO
(719) 634-4098
e-mail: mkantor@usa.net

West River Unschoolers
2420 N. First St.
Grand Junction, CO 81501
(970) 241-4137

Connecticut

Connecticut Home Educators Association
80 Coppermine Rd.
Oxford, CT 06478
(203) 732-0102

CT's CURE (CT's Citizens to Uphold the Right to Educate)
Box 597
Sherman, CT 06784
(203) 355-4724 or (203) 354-3590

The Education Association of Christian Homeschoolers (TEACH)
25 Field Stone Run
Farmington, CT 06032
(800) 205-8744

Unschoolers Support
22 Wildrose Ave.
Guilford, CT 06437
(203) 458-7402

Delaware

DE Home Education Association
Box 1003
Dover, DE 19903

Tri-State Homeschool Network
Box 7193
Newark, DE 19714
(302) 322-2018

Florida

The Family Learning Exchange
2020 Turpentine Rd.
Mims, FL 32754
(407) 268-8833

Florida Parent Educators Association (FPEA)
Box 371
Melbourne, FL 32902
(407) 722-0895
e-mail: office@fpea.com
Web site: www.fpea.com

Home Education Resources and Information (HERI)
711 St. Johns Bluff Rd.
Jacksonville, FL 32225
(904) 565-9121
e-mail: herijax@juno.com

Home Educators Assistance League
3343 Shoal Creek Cove
Crestview, FL 32539
(904) 682-2422

Home Educators Lending Parents Support (HELPS)
5941 NW 14 Ct.
Sunrise, FL 33313
(954) 791-9733
e-mail:
Scapraro-helps@juno.com

Homeschool Network
Box 940402
Maitland, FL 32794
e-mail: forest5@gdi.net

Parkland Home Educators
2045 Houndslake Dr.
Winter Park, FL 32792
(407) 677-1891
e-mail: abercrom@netwide.net

Georgia

Athens Area Homeschoolers
1855 Jot-Em-Down Rd.
Danielsville, GA 30633
(706) 789-2159

Atlanta Alternative Education Network
1586 Rainier Falls Dr.
Atlanta, GA 30329
(404) 636-6348
e-mail:
mickaels@mindspring.com
Web site:
www.mindspring.com/~lei/aaen

Augusta Area Home Education Network (AHN)
3205 Montpelier Dr.
Augusta, GA 30909
e-mail: pstein@worldnet.att.net

Douglas County Home Educators
3855 Jims Ct.
Douglasville, GA 30135
(770) 949-3297

Family Education for Christ
Box 16619
Savannah, GA 31416
(912) 354-5204
e-mail: fefc.savh@juno.com

Free to Learn at Home
4439 Lake Forest Dr.
Oakwood, GA 30566
(770) 536-8077

Georgians for Freedom in Education
7180 Cane Leaf Dr.
Fairburn, GA 30213
(770) 463-1563

LIGHT
Box 2724
Columbus, GA 31902
(706) 324-3714

Parent Educators Association for Children at Home (PEACH)
Box 430
Buford, GA 30515
(770) 969-5872

Hawaii

Christian Homeschoolers of Hawaii
91-824 Oama St.
Ewa Beach, HI 96706
(808) 689-6398

Hawaii Homeschool Association
Box 893476
Mililani, HI 96789
(808) 944-3339
e-mail: TGthrngPlc@aol.com

Kauai Home Educators Association
(808) 245-7867
e-mail: jeanne@aloha.net

Idaho

Family Unschooling Network
1809 N. Seventh St.
Boise, ID 83702
(208) 345-2703
e-mail:
NeysaJensen@CompuServe.com

Palouse Home Learning Alternatives
802 White Ave.
Moscow, ID 83843
(208) 882-1593

Southeast Idaho Homeschool Association
1440 Eastridge
Pocatello, ID 83201
e-mail: joyfuljoyc@aol.com

Illinois

Evanston Home Educators
9508 Springfield Ave.
Evanston, IL 60203
(847) 675-3632
e-mail:
102723.2764@compuserve.com

Home Educated Little People
Rockford, IL
(815) 234-8599
e-mail: traciu1@mwci.net

Homeschooling Answers
806 Oakton
Evanston, IL 60202
(847) 328-7129
e-mail: RichardW@tezcat.com

Homeschooling Families of Illinois
Dupage County, IL
(630) 548-4349

HOUSE
2508 E. 22nd Pl.
Sauk Village, IL 60411
(708) 758-7374
e-mail: ASERET70@aol.com

IL Christian Home Educators
Box 261
Zion, IL 60099
(708) 662-1909

Islamic Homeschooling Education Network
241 Meadowbrook Dr.
Bolingbrook, IL 60440
e-mail: ILYASAH@aol.com

Spectrum Homeschoolers
10859 Longwood Dr.
Chicago, IL 60643-3312
(773) 779-7608

Unschoolers Network
736 N. Mitchell Ave.
Arlington Heights, IL 60004
(847) 253-8902
e-mail: PJADK@aol.com

Indiana

Families Learning Together
1714 E. 51st St.
Indianapolis, IN 46205
(317) 255-9298
e-mail: whelan.mullen@juno.com

Homefront
1120 W. Whiskey Run Ridge
New Salisbury, IN 47161
(812) 347-2931

IN Association of Home Educators
1000 N. Madison #S2
Greenwood, IN 46142
(317) 638-9633

L.E.A.R.N.
9577 E. State Rd. 45
Unionville, IN 47468
(812) 336-8028

Wabash Valley Homeschool Association
Box 3865
Terre Haute, IN 47803
e-mail: WVHA@aol.com

Iowa

IA Home Educators' Association
Box 213
Des Moines, IA 50301

Network of IA Christian Homeschoolers
Box 158
Dexter, IA 50070

Kansas

Circle of Homeschoolers and Unschoolers in Central Kansas
R.R. 1, Box 28A
Rush Center, KS 67575
(913) 372-4457

Heartland Area Homeschooler's Association
823 West St.
Emporia, KS 66801
(316) 343-3696

Konza Homeschoolers Association
319 Knoxberry Dr.
Manhattan, KS 66502
(913) 587-8280

Lawrence Area Unaffiliated Group of Homeschoolers (LAUGH)
R.R. 1, Box 496
Perry, KS 66073
(913) 597-5579

Teaching Parents Association
Box 3968
Wichita, KS 67201
(316) 945-0810

Kentucky

Bluegrass Home Educators
600 Shake Rag Rd.
Waynesburg, KY 40489
e-mail: bhe@ky-on-line.com
Web site: ky-on-line.com/bhe

Kentucky Home Education Association
Box 81
Winchester, KY 40392

KY Independent Learners Network
Box 275
Somerset, KY 42501
(606) 678-2527

Louisiana

Homeschoolers Learning from Mother Earth
14189 Ridge Rd.
Prairieville, LA 70769

Homeschooling Organizing for Progressive Education (HOPE)
5229 Hwy. 3276
Stonewall, LA 71078

Wild Azalea Unschoolers
6055 General Meyer Ave.
New Orleans, LA 70131
(504) 392-5647
e-mail: tws01@gnofn.org

Maine

The Homeschool Support Network
Box 708
Gray, ME 04039
(207) 657-2800
e-mail: hsn@outrig.com
Web site:
www.chfweb.com/hsn/

Homeschoolers of Maine
HC 62, Box 24
Hope, ME 04847
(207) 763-4251

Maine Home Education Association
Box 421
Topsham, ME 04086
(800) 520-0577

Southern Maine Home Education Support Network
76 Beech Ridge Rd.
Scarborough, ME 04074
(207) 883-9621

Maryland

Educating Our Own
686 Geneva Dr.
Westminster, MD 21157
(410) 857-0168 or
(410) 848-3390

Maryland Home Education Association
9805 Flamepool Way
Columbia, MD 21045
(410) 730-0073

Montgomery Home Learning Network
14220 Dennington Pl.
Rockville, MD 20853
(301) 871-6431
e-mail: gyvate@juno.com

North County Home Educators
1688 Belhaven Woods Ct.
Pasadena, MD 21122
(410) 437-5109
e-mail: 2108942@MICmail.com

Prince George's Home Learning Network
3730 Marlbrough Way
College Park, MD 20740
(301) 935-5456 or (301) 431-1838

Massachusetts

The Family Resource Center
Box 308
Salem, MA 01970
(508) 741-7449
e-mail: BigBear001@aol.com

Franklin County Homelearning Families
72 Prospect St.
Greenfield, MA 01301
(413) 773-9280

The HOME Club
19 Florence St.
Cambridge, MA 02139
(617) 876-7273

Homeschooling Together
24 Avon Pl.
Arlington, MA 02474
e-mail: ses@world.std.com
Web site: people.ne.media
one.net/jrsladkey/hst

Jewish Homeschoolers of Massachusetts
e-mail: FernReiss@aol.com

MA Homeschoolers Organization of Parent Educators
15 Ohio St.
Wilmington, MA 01887
(508) 658-8970

Massachusetts Home Learning Association
Box 1558
Marstons Mills, MA 02648
(508) 429-1436
e-mail: LorettaMCH@aol.com

Merrimack Valley Homelearners Group
13 Ashdale Rd.
N. Billerica, MA 01862
(508) 663-2755
e-mail: garyd@chelmsford.com

Michigan

Celebrating Home Under Rome—Catholic Homeschoolers (CHURCH)
(517) 349-6389
e-mail: RWittLans@aol.com

Families Learning and Schooling at Home
21671 B Drive N.
Marshall, MI 49068
(616) 781-1069

HELP—Michigan
125 E. Lincoln
Negaunee, MI 49866
(906) 475-5508

Heritage Home Educators
13339 Firestone Ct.
Fenton, MI 48430

Hillsdale Area Homeschoolers
5151 Barker Rd.
Jonesville, MI 49250
(517) 287-5565

Home Educators Circle
1280 John Hix St.
Westland, MI 48186
(313) 326-4206

The Homeschool Support Network
Box 2457
Riverview, MI 48192
(313) 284-1249

Older Homeschoolers' Group
9120 Dwight Dr.
Detroit, MI 48214
(313) 331-8406

Minnesota

MN Association of Roman Catholic Home Educators
7211 Sherwood Echo
Woodbury, MN 55125
(612) 730-8101

MN Homeschoolers Alliance
Box 23072
Richfield, MN 55423
(612) 491-2828

Mississippi

Coast Military Home Educators
9212A Givens Circle
Biloxi, MS 39531
(601) 388-4522

Home Educators of Central Mississippi
535 Luling St.
Pearl, MS 39208

MS Home Educators Association
R.R. 9, Box 350
Laurel, MS 39440-8720

Missouri

Families for Home Education
400 E. High Point Lane
Columbia, MO 65203
(816) 826-9302

LEARN
Box 10105
Kansas City, MO 64171
(913) 383-7888

Ozark Lore Society
HC 73, Box 160
Drury, MO 65638
(417) 679-3391
e-mail: deb@wiseheart.com

Springfield Home Education
Box 1412
Springfield, MO 65801
(417) 862-0520
e-mail:
cwaddell@mail.orion.org

St. Louis Homeschool Network
4147 W. Pine
St. Louis, MO 63108
(314) 534-1171

Montana

Bozeman Homeschool Network
201 S. Sixth St., Apt. A
Bozeman, MT 59715
(406) 586-3499
e-mail: dalton@ycsi.net

Independent Homeschoolers Network of Bozeman
415 S. Ninth Ave.
Bozeman, MT 59715
(406) 586-4564

Mid-Mountain Home Education Network
Box 2182
Montana City Station, MT 59634
(406) 443-3376

Montana Coalition of Home Educators
Box 654
Helena, MT 59624

Nebraska

LEARN
7741 E. Avon Lane
Lincoln, NE 68505
(402) 488-7741

Nevada

Home Schools United
Box 93564
Las Vegas, NV 89193
(702) 870-9566
e-mail: HSU.VEGAS
VALLEY@juno.com

Homeschool Melting Pot
1778 Antelope Valley Ave.
Henderson, NV 89012
(702) 269-9101
e-mail: barcus@lvcm.com
Web site: www.angelfire.com/
nv/homeschoolmeltingpot/

Northern Nevada Home Schools, Inc.
Box 21323
Reno, NV 89515
(702) 852-6647
e-mail: NNHS@aol.com

New Hampshire

Homeschooling Friends
204 Brackett Rd.
New Durham, NH 03855
(603) 332-4146
e-mail:
nathome@worldpath.net
Web site: www.geocities.com/
Heartland/Plains/9175/

New Hampshire Alliance for Home Education
17 Preserve Dr.
Nashua, NH 03060
(603) 880-8629

New Hampshire Homeschooling Coalition
Box 2224
Concord, NH 03304
(603) 539-7233
Web site:
www.nhhomeschooling.org

New Jersey

Educational Excellence—School at Home
Box 771
Summit, NJ 07901
e-mail: KindPals@aol.com

Homeschoolers of South New Jersey
1239 Whitaker Ave.
Millville, NJ 08332
(609) 327-1224
e-mail: Tutor@Pulsar.net
Web site: www.pulsar.net/~tutor

Unschoolers Network
2 Smith St.
Farmingdale, NJ 07727
(732) 938-2473

Unschooling Families Support Group of Central New Jersey
150 Falwell Station Rd.
Jobstown, NJ 08041
(609) 723-1524

New Mexico

Carlsbad Family Educators
22 Comance Dr.
Carlsbad, NM 88220
(505) 887-6229

Corpus Christi Catholic Home Educators
150 Valle Chaparral
Cedar Crest, NM 87008
(505) 256-4345

East Mountain Family Educators
Box 369
Tijeras, NM 87059
(505) 281-3865

Home Educators of Dona Ana
2202 Rubina Ct.
Las Cruces, NM 88005
(505) 525-2358

Home Educators of Santa Fe
21 Frasco Rd.
Santa Fe, NM 87505
(505) 466-4462
e-mail: McLeod@sfol.com

Homeschooling PACT
Box 961
Portales, NM 88130
(505) 359-1618

New Mexico Family Educators
Box 92276
Albuquerque, NM 87199
(505) 275-7053

Socorro Association of Family Educators
1208 Drake NW
Socorro, NM 87801
(505) 835-0497

Unschoolers of Albuquerque
8116 Princess Jeanne NE
Albuquerque, NM 87110
(505) 299-2476
e-mail: SandraDodd@aol.com

New York

Columbia County Homeschooling Mothers Group
29 Kinderhook St.
Chatham, NY 12037
(518) 392-4277

Families for Home Education
3219 Coulter Rd.
Cazenovia, NY 13035
(315) 655-2574

Fingerlakes Unschoolers Network
201 Elm St.
Ithaca, NY 14850
(607) 273-6257
e-mail: Laundress@aol.com

Independent Home Educators of the Hudson Valley
904 Rte. 9
Staatsburg, NY 12580
(914) 889-4682

New York City Home Educators Alliance
8 E. Second St.
New York, NY 10003
(212) 505-9884
e-mail: RTricamo@aol.com

Oneida Lake Area Home Educators
Box 24
Sylvan Beach, NY 13157
(315) 762-5166

Oneonta Area Sharing in Homeschooling (OASIS)
Box 48
Gilbertsville, NY 13776
(607) 783-2271

Rochester Area Homeschoolers Association
275 Yarmouth Rd.
Rochester, NY 14610
(716) 234-0298

Tri-County Homeschoolers
Box 190
Ossining, NY 10562
(914) 941-5607
e-mail: chofer@croton.com
Web site:
www.croton.com/home-ed/

Tri Lakes Community Home Educators
Box 270
Raybrook, NY 12977
(518) 891-5657

Western New York Homeschoolers
18 Maple Ave.
Portville, NY 14770
(716) 933-8669

North Carolina

Families Learning Together
1670 NC Hwy. 33W
Chocowinity, NC 27817

Holt and Friends Home Education Association
4775 Shattalon Circle
Winston-Salem, NC 27106
e-mail: SARAHCAROTHERS
@prodigy.net
Web site: www.geocities.com/
~holtandfriends

North Carolinians for Home Education
419 N. Boylan Ave.
Raleigh, NC 27603
(919) 834-6243

North Dakota

ND Home School Association
4007 N. State St.
Bismarck, ND 58501
(701) 223-4080

Ohio

Families Independently Schooling at Home (FISH)
Box 266
Polk, OH 44866
Ashland County: (419) 945-2319
Richland County: (419) 747-7286
Wayne County: (330) 262-4489
e-mail: somefish@usa.net

Families Unschooling in the Neighborhood
4132 Spring Flower Ct.
Gahanna, OH 43230
(614) 794-2171
e-mail: roy@qn.net

Families Unschooling in the Neighborhood—Mid Ohio
5668 Township Rd. 105
Mount Gilead, OH 43338
(419) 947-6351
e-mail: laurie@redbird.net

HEART
7979 Greenwich Rd.
Lodi, OH 44254
(330) 948-2941
e-mail: zcarter@apk.net

HELP—Central Ohio
4132 Spring Flower Ct.
Gahanna, OH 43230
(614) 470-2219
e-mail: roy@qn.net

HELP—Northern Ohio
10915 Pyle—S. Amherst Rd.
Oberlin, OH 44074
(216) 774-2720

HELP—Northwest Ohio
Box 98
Perrysburg, OH 43552
(419) 478-9729 or
(419) 476-1088

Home Education Resource Organization
170 W. Main St.
Norwalk, OH 44857
(419) 663-1064

Home Educators Advocacy League
348 Cobblestone Dr.
Delaware, OH 43015
(614) 369-4706

Homeschool Network of Greater Cincinnati
3470 Greenfield Ct.
Maineville, OH 45039
(513) 683-1279 or
(513) 772-9579

Ohio Home Educators Network
Box 23054
Chagrin Falls, OH 44023
(330) 278-2540
e-mail: buresmom@aol.com

Parents and Children Together (PACT)
8944 Weiss Rd.
Union City, OH 45390
(937) 692-5680 or (937) 968-4942

Youngstown Home Learners
266 Outlook Ave.
Youngstown, OH 44504
(330) 744-5376
e-mail: Ytownpam@aol.com

Oklahoma

Cornerstone
Box 459
Sperry, OK 74073
(918) 425-4162

Green County Home Educators Resource Organization
183 Fox Run Circle
Jenks, OK 74037

Home Educators Resource Organization
302 N. Coolidge
Enid, OK 73703
(580) 438-2253
e-mail: mjmiller@pldi.ne
Web site: www.geocities.com/
Athens/Forum/3236/

Oregon

Greater Portland Homeschoolers
Box 82415
Portland, OR 97282
(503) 241-5350
e-mail: Schertzkat@aol.com

Homeschool Information and Service Network
1044 Bismark
Klamath Falls, OR 97601

Oregon Christian Home Education Association
2515 N.E. 37th Ave.
Portland, OR 97212

Oregon Home Education Network
4470 S.W. Hall Blvd. #286
Beaverton, OR 97005
(503) 321-5166
e-mail: sassenak@teleport.com
Web site:
www.teleport.com/~ohen

Pennsylvania

Blue Mountain Homeschoolers
636 Almond Road
Walnutport, PA 18088

Bucks County Homeschoolers
125 Mountain Oaks Rd.
Yardley, PA 19067
(215) 428-3865
e-mail: renee321@juno.com

Catholic Homeschoolers of Scranton
1317 St. Ann St.
Scranton, PA 18504
(717) 334-8866

Center City Homeschoolers
2203 Spruce St.
Philadelphia, PA 19103
(215) 732-7723 or (215) 482-7933

Diversity—United in Homeschooling
233 Blue Bell Ave.
Langhorne, PA 19407
(215) 428-2865

Homeschoolers Association of Warren County
R.R. 1, Box 87B1
Youngsville, PA 16371
(814) 489-3366
e-mail: Cyndi@Penn.com

Maryland/Pennsylvania Home Educators
Box 67
Shrewsbury, PA 17361
(717) 993-3603 or (717) 993-2962

McKeesport Area Homeschoolers
404 Owens Ave.
Liberty Borough, PA
(412) 672-7056
e-mail: pageclan@msn.com

Pennsylvania Home Education Network
285 Allegheny St.
Meadville, PA 16335
(412) 561-5288

People Always Learning Something (PALS)
105 Marie Dr.
Pittsburgh, PA 15237
(412) 367-6240

Southwestern PA Home Education Network
429 Union Ave.
Pittsburgh, PA 15205
(412) 922-8344

Valley Unschoolers Network
4458 Coffeetown Rd.
Schneckville, PA 18078
(610) 799-2742

Rhode Island

Parent Educators of Rhode Island
Box 782
Glendale, RI 02826

Rhode Island Guild of Home Teachers (RIGHT)
Box 11
Hope, RI 02831
(401) 821-7700
e-mail:
right_right@mailexcite.com
Web site: www.angelfire.com/
ri/RIGHT/

South County Homeschoolers
500 Carolina Back Rd.
Charleston, RI 02813

South Carolina

Home Organization of Parent Educators
1697 Dotterer's Run
Charleston, SC 29414
(803) 763-7833
e-mail: epeeler@awod.com

SC Association of Independent Home Schools
Box 2014
Irmo, SC 29063-2104

SC Home Educators Association
Box 612
Lexington, SC 29071

The South Carolina Homeschool Alliance
1679 Memorial Park Rd.
Suite 179
Lancaster, SC 29720
e-mail: ConnectSC@aol.com

South Carolina Homeschool Support Group
242 Weathers Farm Rd.
Bowman, SC 29018
(803) 563-9322

Teacher's Ink
Box 13386
Charleston, SC 29422
(803) 795-9982
e-mail: pfmsuper@worldnet.att.net

Tri-County Educational Association of Community Homeschoolers (TEACH)
107 Prairie Lane
Summerville, SC 29483
(803) 871-6683
e-mail: Mooooom@aol.com

South Dakota

South Dakota Home School Association
Box 882
Sioux Falls, SD 57101
(605) 338-9689

Tennessee

State of Franklin Homeschoolers
494 Mill Creek Rd.
Kingsport, TN 37664
(423) 349-6125
e-mail: kramerbg@mounet.com

Tennessee Homeschooling Families
214 Park Lane
Oliver Springs, TN 37840
(423) 435-9644

Texas

Austin Area Homeschoolers
510 Park Blvd.
Austin, TX 78751

Heart of Texas Home Schoolers
1710 Vincent
Brownwood, TX 76801
(915) 643-1182
e-mail: charlotte@gte.net

Highland Lake Area Homeschoolers
Rte. 1, Box 239
Burnet, TX 78611
(512) 756-2982
e-mail: tolliver@tstar.net

Houston Alternative Education Alliance
14222 Ridgewood Lake Ct.
Houston, TX 77062
(713) 667-7837

Houston Unschoolers Group
9625 Exeter Rd.
Houston, TX 77093
(713) 695-4888
e-mail: MHFurgason@Hotmail.com

Learning and Education Alternatives Resource Network (LEARN)
Box 176
Arlington, TX 76004
e-mail: deblewis@fastlane.net

North Texas Self Educators
150 Forest Lane
Double Oak/Lewisville, TX 75067
(817) 430-4835

South Fort Worth Christian Home Educators
Box 16573
Fort Worth, TX 76133
(817) 249-1975 or
(817) 923-3451
e-mail: robbjh@flash.net

South Texas Self-Learners
1005 Delta Dr.
Corpus Christi, TX 78412
(512) 992-7549

Southwest Dallas Home School Association
Box 1104
Cedar Hill, TX 75106
e-mail: StoryLadee@aol.com

Tarrant Home Educators Association
6080 Hulen Dr.
Suite 360-109
Fort Worth, TX 76132
(817) 421-1761

Wharton County Christian Homeschool Organization
Box 1411
El Campo, TX 77437
(409) 543-1999
e-mail: car@wcnet.net

Utah

HELP—Four Corners
Castle Valley Star Rte., Box 1901
Moab, UT 84532
(801) 259-6968

Latter-Day Saints Home Educators Association
2770 S. 1000 W
Perry, UT
(801) 723-5355

Utah Home Education Association
Box 167
Roy, UT 84067
(888) 887-UHEA
Web site:
www.itsnet.com/~uhea

Vermont

Christian Home Educators of Vermont
214 N. Prospect St., #105
Burlington, VT 05401
(802) 658-4561
e-mail: GESA97@aol.com

The Resource Center for Homeschooling
R.R. 2, Box 289C
St. Albans, VT 05478
(802) 524-9645
e-mail: shell@together.net

Right at Home
R.R. 2, Box 145
E. Wallingford, VT 05742
(802) 259-3493
e-mail:
cwade@vermontel.com

Vermont Homeschoolers Association
R.R. 2, Box 4440
Bristol, VT 05443
(802) 453-5460

United Homeschoolers
R.R. 1, Box 47B
South Royalton, VT 05068
(802) 763-2837
e-mail: dltimian@together.net

Virginia

Blue Ridge Area Network for Congenial Homeschoolers
255 Ipswich Pl.
Charlottesville, VA 22901
(804) 974-7149
e-mail: amy@pcsp.com

Children's Circle
R.R. 1, Box 132A
Mouth of Wilson, VA 24363
(703) 579-4252

Community of Independent Learners
Box 16029
Alexandria, VA 22302

Family Oriented Learning Cooperative
1441 F St.
Woodbridge, VA 22191
(703) 494-6021 or
(703) 497-2873
e-mail:
ShirleeSeaborne@juno.com

Fauquier Unschoolers Living Classroom
Box 51
Goldvein, VA 22720
(540) 752-2478

Home Educators Are Restoring Their Heritage (HEARTH)
Box 69
Linden, VA 22642
(540) 636-3713
e-mail:
chrisd@juddsonline.com
Web site: www.shentel.net/
revival/hearth.htm

**Home Educators Assisting,
Reaching, and Teaching
(HEART)**
101 William Claiborne
Williamsburg, VA 23185
(757) 220-2052
e-mail:
BIZIMOM807@aol.com

**LEARN—Northern Virginia
Homeschoolers**
1111 Waynewood Blvd.
Alexandria, VA 22308

**Learning in a Family
Environment**
40672 Tankerville Rd.
Lovettsville, VA 20180
e-mail: ebarkan@aol.com

**Lifespan Education and Resource
Network**
3703 Merrimac Trail
Annandale, VA 22003
(703) 569-3264
e-mail: DramaDeb@aol.com

**Richmond Educational
Alternatives for Children at
Home (REACH)**
Box 36174
Richmond, VA 23235
(804) 795-7624
e-mail:
carmel@compuserve.com
Web site: www.geocities.com/
Heartland/Plains/7440/

**Virginia Home Education
Association**
1612 Columbia Rd.
Gordonsville, VA 22942
(540) 832-3578
e-mail: vhea@virginia.edu
Web site: poe.acc.virginia.edu/
~pm6f/vhea/html

WELCOME
108 Fardale St. SE
Vienna, VA 22180
(703) 573-7121
e-mail: Markoff@dcnet.com

Washington

Family Learning Organization
Box 7247
Spokane, WA 99207
(509) 924-3760 or (509) 467-2552

Fun Family Homeschool Group
421 N.E. 12th St.
North Bend, WA 98045
e-mail: fisler@msn.com

**Home Educators Cooperative of
the Mid-Columbia**
41005 E. Hacienda
Benton City, WA 99320
(509) 967-3301 or
(509) 588-3861
e-mail: BrittMak@aol.com

**Homeschoolers Support
Association**
Box 413
Maple Valley, WA 98038
(425) 746-5047

**Network of Vancouver Area
Homeschoolers**
162 Krogstad Rd.
Washougal, WA 98671
(360) 837-3760
e-mail: 71230.66@compuserve.com

**North Central Washington
Homeschool Coop**
Box 147
Curlew, WA 99118

Peninsula Homeschool Exchange
419 Benton St.
Port Townsend, WA 98368
(360) 385-3830

St. Thomas Moore Home Education
3853 76th Ave. SE
Mercer Island, WA 98040
(206) 232-2680

Seattle Homeschool Group
8725 14th Ave. NW
Seattle, WA 98117
e-mail:
shgnewsletter@hotmail.com

Teaching Parents Association
Box 1934
Woodinville, WA 98072
(425) 739-8562 or
(425) 844-3047

Valley Home Educators
1413 Easthills Terr.
E. Wenatchee, WA 98802
(509) 884-1237

Washington Homeschool Organization
6632 S. 191st Pl.
Suite E100
Kent, WA 98032
(425) 251-0439
e-mail:
WHOoffice@juno.com
Web site:
www.washhomeschool.org

West Virginia

West Virginia Home Educators Association
Box 3707
Charleston, WV 25337
(800) 736-9843
e-mail: wvhea@bigfoot.com
Web site:
members.tripod.com/~WVHEA

Wisconsin

HOME
5745 Bittersweet Pl.
Madison, WI 53705
(608) 238-3302
e-mail:
amckee73@hotmail.com

Home Scholars of Sheboygan County
W5607 Hwy. W
Adell, WI 53001
(920) 528-7057
e-mail: darcymz@execpc.com

La Crosse Educational Alternative Resource Network
W. 6442 Schilling Rd.
Onalaska, WI 54650

Milwaukee Area Home Learners
W260 N7751 Jay Lane
Sussex, WI 53089
(414) 246-3604

Ozaukee Explorers
4410 Bittersweet Lane
Cedarburg, WI 53210
(414) 377-7734
e-mail: PIPENN@aol.com

Wisconsin Parents Association
Box 2502
Madison, WI, 53701

Wyoming

Homeschoolers of Wyoming
Box 926
Evansville, WY 82636

Unschoolers of Wyoming/Laramie Home Education Network
429 Hwy. 230, #20
Laramie, WY 82010

INDEX